Natural Cat

BY LISA S. NEWMAN, N.D., Ph.D.

Foreword by Deborah C. Mallu, D.V.M., C.V.A.

THE CROSSING PRESS
FREEDOM, CALIFORNIA

For information on bulk purchases or group discounts for this and other Crossing Press titles, please contact our Special Sales Manager at 800/777-1048.

Visit our website on the Internet: **www.crossingpress.com**

Cautionary Note: The nutritional information, recipes, and instructions contained within this book are in no way intended as a substitute for medical counseling. Please do not attempt self-treatment of a medical problem without consulting a qualified health practitioner.

The author and The Crossing Press expressly disclaim any and all liability for any claims, damages, losses, judgments, expenses, costs, and liabilities of any kind or injuries resulting from any products offered in this book by particing companies and their employees or agents. Nor does the inclusion of any resource group or company listed within this book constitute an endorsement or guarantee of quality by the author or The Crossing Press.

ISBN 1-58091-001-7

Library of Congress Cataloging-in-Publication Data

Newman, Lisa S.
    Natural cat / by Lisa S. Newman.
        p. cm. -- (The Crossing Press pocket series)
    At head of title: Natural pet care.
    ISBN 1-58091-001-7 (pbk.)
    1. Cats. 2. Cats--Health. 3. Cats--Diseases--Alternative treatment. 4. Holistic veterinary medicine. I. Title. II. Title: Natural pet care. III. Series.
SF447.N496   1999
636.8'0893--dc21   99-37385
                                                                          CIP

Contents

Foreword

It is with great pleasure that I introduce Lisa Newman's remarkable series. She has dedicated her life to helping you care for your animal companions—we can all benefit from her years of experience.

We are living in a time of great change, especially in the realm of health care. As a practicing veterinarian for more than two decades, I have witnessed both myself and my clients begin to seek less invasive, more natural methods for healing our dogs and cats. Once we understood that all beings are interconnected on this planet, we became aware that our thoughts, emotions, and family dynamics played an important role in the health of our animal companions. We began to realize the importance of forming a team first with the members of our animal family, aided by other healing professionals including natural health counselors and animal communicators.

Over the years I have heard people say, "I didn't know you could use that natural remedy or treatment on animals." Feel confident that you can help your animal companions where the healing is best—in your loving home. Our animals nurture us by giving us unconditional love. In turn, we can nurture them with fresh, live food and supplements, so that they can live a long and healthy life. Lisa Newman will show you the way so that you can be empowered as a healer.

Deborah C. Mallu, D.V.M., C.V.A.

Introduction

Cats are either our little angels or devils. They can give us their love without reservation—yet they think nothing of ignoring our presence to the point of driving us mad. They are driven to love and obey us, even forgive us as we mistreat them—or see right through us. In turn, we shelter, tend, and feed them, allow them into our hearts, and grieve their passing. As families become more transient, pets play an even more important role in maintaining our sense of belonging. Whether in relationships or living alone (due to choice, age, or debility) people benefit from the daily contact and sense of purpose a cat provides. It is a complex yet basic relationship, one that nourishes our physical, emotional, and spiritual well-being.

Raising a cat has become more complex over the years. Genetic problems (such as immune deficiencies, digestive disorders, and neurological problems) have been bred into the gene pool. Environmental pollutants and chemicals in cats' diets and even in their drinking water have further weakened them. Since cats reproduce at a considerably faster rate than we do, we have had several generations to study them, and the results are frightening. Regardless of the medical advances in veterinary care, the development of premium "scientific" or "natural" diets, and the improvement in how we treat our pets—they are sicker than ever.

Concerned owners spend hundreds, if not thousands, of dollars suppressing various health or behavioral conditions, many of them chronic. Each cycle of symptoms or accidents mounts a new campaign of drugs, shampoos, creams, and supplements, not to mention changes in diets and handling. While many changes do temporarily suppress the discomfort of the symptoms, the condition gradually gets worse. As cats

7

get older, their resistance to disease weakens, and their symptoms become more difficult to treat. This cycle—of suppression of symptoms and symptom recurrence once medication has stopped—is all too familiar for many pets and their caregivers. A holistic lifestyle through diet, supplementation of nutrients and herbs, homeopathic remedies, exercise, communication (teaching without trauma), and proper grooming can play an important role in providing your cat with optimum health and emotional wellness.

The principles of holistic animal care as described in this book should not be used in lieu of, but as support to, proper veterinary care. This book is not intended to diagnose illness, prescribe medical treatment, make any claims, or imply any guarantees. I feel that sharing information on the proven, non-medical, safe, natural alternatives available to your pet will help you provide them with optimum care.

Please inform your veterinarian of any serious health concerns and observations you may have. Do rely on your vet's clinical diagnoses, blood work, x-rays, and medication when needed. Above all, please honor yourself and your animals. Trust in what you observe or sense, but continue to examine all sides of any issue. There are many sources of information available, but it is up to you to decide what is best for you and your cat.

I also want to encourage you to follow primarily a holistic course of treatment even when your pet is seriously ill. My goal is to take the mystery out of raising your cat as nature intended—by identifying safe, effective feeding, training, and care procedures, including natural symptom relief.

The Natural Cat

Today's cat breeds are the result of intense domestication and increasing genetic manipulation, resulting in many cats now struggling with physical or behavioral issues. Certain breeds have become popular at different times, such as the Persian, Tonkinese, or Maine Coon cat. Other breeds have become popular because of the movies: the honorable Siamese, the adorable Calico, or the regal Russian Blue. Such specialization has changed the genetic codes in favor of appearance, size, and color, but has also mutated the genetic information for health and emotional stability. As a result, many pet owners are presently faced with health and behavior problems in their cats.

Inbreeding and excessive genetic manipulation has minimized our animals' natural ability to cure themselves. Moreover, years of vaccinations, chemical baths, flea/tick potions, dips or sprays, medications, and most importantly, the poor-quality ingredients, artificial colors, preservatives, and by-products found in most pet foods and treats eventually take their toll.

Cancer, especially feline leukemia, is one of the most dreaded diseases today, along with premature aging. Both conditions are often preceded by a long history of neglected or suppressed symptoms. Whether these symptoms are considered isolated—or the result of a specific disease or organ failure—over ninety-five percent of these symptoms are preventable with proper care. Behavioral issues are also on the rise, as more cats exhibit aggressive or fearful attitudes and have trouble learning to get along with their human families. Although many breeds are predisposed towards these behaviors, they are more likely to be triggered by chemicals and sugar in their diet, and by early experiences of abandonment or mistreatment. It is obvious then, that these behaviors are preventable, regardless of "poor" genetics. This is what holistic animal care is all about: to help you support the most positive genetic potential your cat has, and thus to prevent or reverse problems.

UNDERSTANDING YOUR CAT'S BEHAVIOR

Cats can be very difficult to understand at times. If left alone, they demand to be noticed. If given attention, some cats prefer to ignore us. Unlike dogs who crave close connection with their human family, cats appear to be quite happy spending their time alone. Yet, paradoxically, they will become stressed when they feel abandoned, and their distress can manifest as behavioral or physical symptoms.

The majority of behavioral problems are created by miscommunication—you and your cat are speaking two different languages. Imagine for a moment that you are in a foreign land trying to understand your tour guide, who doesn't speak English. What a relief it is when you work out some familiar signals. Cats are looking at us constantly for such signals, trying to decipher what we are saying, because they desperately want to please us. Begin to understand your cat by putting yourself in his or her paws.

Ask yourself if your cat can rely on:

- **Your love**—consistent, fair and gentle; focused and sincere
- **Your attention**—daily regard as to their emotional and physical well-being
- **Your care**—responsive to disorder, accident, or illness (acute or long-term)
- **Your home**—a safe and loving shelter; free of fear or stress
- **Your devotion**—through the easy times *and* the difficult ones

Exploring and changing certain things to fit your cat's needs rather than your own, caring for their well-being, and raising them well can prevent a lot of struggle on both your parts.

TRAINING WITHOUT TRAUMA

You should never raise your hand to a kitten or cat—they will only think that you are attacking them. Most people hit their cat out of frustration due to poor communication. Cats learn by repetition. It takes approximately fifty repetitions, hearing the command and correctly associating the desired behavior with that command, before you can rely on the fact that your cat *understands* and is not simply reacting to you.

Be absolutely clear and consistent in the signals you are giving your cat:

- Do not say "get away" one time and "no" the next—use "No!" only as NO! and mean it.

- Do not use "NO" indiscriminately—your cat will simply become deaf to it.

- Give a warning "NO!" If behavior continues, say it in a lower voice with more growl-tones.

- A shot of water from a spray bottle or water pistol, *at the moment of sin*, does work.

- As a second warning grab the loose skin on back of neck and jerk it slightly. This method of discipline should be used immediately if biting or scratching is involved. Also, keeping your fingers, hand, or arm in the cat's mouth until they try to get away will quickly take the fun out of their "attacking" you. *Do not hurt them, just frustrate them!*

- As a third and final warning, grab the cat by the back of the collar or loose skin and hold them into submission for ten seconds (count it off). Cats hate being "held back." They will quickly do what is needed to regain freedom.

- If behavior escalates—then isolate the cat in a quiet place, no longer than fifteen minutes or they will forget they were "banished"—allow them back into the fold without fanfare.

This method of discipline closely resembles the way a queen will discipline her kittens—the way the kitten (or cat) is "wired." (It's their language.) Therefore, a cat will quickly respond and understand that what they did was not acceptable behavior. There is no need to chase the cat, screaming and hitting them, or ignoring them until the problem gets worse—possibly to the point of no return.

To help your cat understand and develop a fondness for learning from you:

- Do not play or work with your cat when you are in a bad mood or short-tempered.
- Begin each session with play or exercise, which will focus your cat and let off steam.
- Always use the same signals and commands—follow the same routine.
- Set aside time each day to practice communicating together by working together.
- Understand for yourself *first* what you will teach—*then* teach it.
- Go over a new command until the cat learns it perfectly. Do this before you begin to teach your cat a new command. This builds confidence in you and in your cat. Confusion will quickly erode effective communication.
- Always end training sessions with a few minutes of exercise/ play/fun.
- End the session with your cat eager to continue learning, not freaked out.

Taking the time to properly communicate with your cat through a "common" language will provide you with a better, more reliable companion. A trained cat is less likely to be destructive, to run off and get hit by a car, to hurt another pet or human, or to develop bad habits—because you are connecting with your cat and correcting bad habits. Because your cat is pleasant and fun to be around, you will be spending more time with her. Consequently, your trained cat is less likely to get sick.

The most important thing to teach your cat is how to be handled. Trained cats can be picked up and held or kenneled indefinitely without stress. They do not mind being put in a carrier for transportation or riding in a moving vehicle. They do not mind being examined by you or any other person. Your cat must allow you to hold them. You must be able to touch all parts of their bodies, look inside their ears or mouth, and do anything else that might need to be done if they are hurt or ill. If your cat is afraid of being held and examined, the fear can do more harm than the injury or illness itself.

NOAH'S THEORY

I have long advocated that cats should be raised in twos since they are such active animals and we as primary friends are often not available to them—especially late at night when they prefer to play. A kitty pal can keep another cat from going crazy and acting out, or becoming ill from turning the loneliness inward. If you have more than two cats, you run the risk of not having enough of yourself to go around. I say—never have more cats than you can pet yourself—at the same time! I should mention that getting another cat as companion for your cat cannot substitute for your love and attention. You will have to care for both, and the more time and attention you give to two cats, the greater the payoff—you will have two well-behaved cats, rather than one neurotic one.

There is, of course, a downside to having more than one cat. If you can't afford or don't have time to feed and care for two, don't get a second cat—you will hurt both yourself and your cats. If you can afford the time, money, and energy, but you do not have a lot of time for your cat during the week—please consider getting another, so they can have each other's company. Although there may be a lot of "fur static" and hissing initially, most cats adjust to each other quickly if not forced together. Never force any issues with a cat or they will emotionally retreat from the unpleasant situation. They are not as forgiving as a dog, so plan new changes carefully.

The more time and attention that you take in understanding your cat and his or her needs, the easier it will be to prevent behavioral issues from ruining your relationship. A happy, well-adjusted cat is one who is less likely to suffer from disease. Emotional stress can have as much to do with immune dysfunction and the manifestation of symptoms as diet can. A cat who is fed the very best diet and is nutritionally supplemented, but lives a fearful or stressful life will have trouble assimilating nutrients and maintaining good health. Providing a loving, stable home will help support your cat's well-being as much as anything else you can do.

Holistic Animal Care

Holistic animal care addresses the entire body rather than its parts, encompassing the body, mind, spirit, and even the environment. The application of various modalities is done in a synergistic way to help stimulate, strengthen, and support the body's own biological processes and natural defenses. This care is used as a means of preventing as well as reversing biological imbalances, which can lead to health or behavioral problems.

Nutrition is central to holistic animal care. It can often be the deciding factor between emotional wellness, health, and disease. Poor nutrition will quickly lead to an imbalance, cripple the body's curative abilities, and possibly create behavioral problems. Regardless of the amount of attention, drugs, or natural remedies given to cats, if they are not receiving adequate nutrition, their own curative response is hindered.

Nutrition is also the cornerstone of a modality known as naturopathy. Defined by a medical dictionary as a "drugless system of therapy by the use of physical forces, such as air, light, water, heat, massage, etc.," naturopathy emphasizes supporting the body's physical attempts to eliminate disease. Naturopaths believe that a major cause of disease is an excessive build-up of toxic materials (often due to improper eating and lack of exercise) which clog the eliminatory system. Various techniques are used to detoxify and stimulate the body, so that symptoms and disease are reversed. Cats are put on supportive programs of high-quality nutrition, proper food combining (to stimulate and aid digestion), and the judicious use of nutritional supplements and herbs. Prevention is considered the best cure.

Basic to folk medicine and every culture since ancient times, herbs are probably the oldest known remedies that are used to stimulate healing. It is widely believed that people began using herbs after observing how animals in the wild would instinctively select appropriate herbs when they are ill. In herbology, leaves, roots, bark, flowers, and seeds are used to assist the healing process primarily by helping the body to eliminate and to detoxify. Herbs provide a slower and deeper action than prescription drugs. They are quickly becoming mainstream, with a growing presence in regular drug stores and supermarket chains.

Another modality, which provides an even slower and deeper action, is homeopathy. Sometimes nutrition or herbs won't be enough—they may begin the cleansing process and support the body (by strengthening it so that it can go through the necessary curative process), but often it is the homeopathic remedy that stimulates the deeper level of healing. The real beauty of the homeopathic system lies in the simplicity of its basic principles and in the safety of its remedies, which have been exhaustively researched and used successfully for hundreds of years.

The German physician, Samuel Hahnemann, founded homeopathy based on one basic principle that has held true ever since homeopathy originated in the late 1700s: that like is cured by like—that a substance that can mimic symptoms can cure them as well. This principle has revolutionized the understanding of symptoms and disease.

Hahnemann noted certain similarities between symptoms produced by some diseases and by the very drugs used to treat them. From this he formed his "Law of Similars," which identified the principle that a disease could be cured by whatever medicine produced similar symptoms when given to a healthy person. The point of homeopathy is that the treatment works with, rather than against, the body's own efforts to regain health.

Bee venom is an example of how homeopathy works. We know that a bee sting will cause a topical reaction, including swelling, fluid accumulation, redness of the skin, pain, and soreness, a reaction that is accentuated by heat or pressure. Some sensitive animals will also experience such behavioral symptoms as apathy, stupor, listlessness, or the opposite, whining and fear. When a homeopathically prepared dilute solution of the venom (known as Apis) is given to a pet with these symptoms—even if they are caused by something other than a bee sting—the condition will soon begin to clear up. The essential key is that the symptoms are quite similar to what the remedy, in its undiluted state, would create.

Flower essences (which balance emotional states) and tissue cell salts (which support physiological processes) act similarly, by stimulating the body's own natural healing and re-establishing homeostasis.

THE HOLISTIC CAT

I define a holistically reared cat to be in a state of balance existing on three interrelated levels: the physical, the emotional, and the environmental. A healthy cat has vitality and is free from physiological malfunction, possesses emotional clarity resulting in good behavior and happiness, and receives (as well as contributes) joy, love, and security in their living environment.

This is the opposite of a chemically reared cat, who is often in a state of imbalance or dis-ease. This cat suffers from chronic symptoms and lacks vitality. Such a cat is generally unbalanced, with a body that is constantly assaulted by substances that a healthy cat would have no problem processing: toxins, allergens, viruses, bacteria, and worms.

Every person who owns a cat should in truth be a caregiver, helping her or his pet's natural curative process—rather than merely suppressing the cat's symptoms, which are simply evidence of the animal's imbalance. The premise of holistic animal care is this: Treat the body well and the body will be well. By providing your cat with ample love, quality nutrition, proper supplementation, and holistic modalities when appropriate, your cat will remain balanced. If certain substances then assault the cat, its innate ability to cure itself will kick in, restoring balance.

UNDERSTANDING THE UNHEALTHY CAT

Most cats that are chronically ill are suffering the long-term consequences of exposure to an emotionally and/or physically toxic environment as well as the cat's ingestion of chemicals. Chemicals alter the primary biological functions in the body, place undue stress on the vital organs and glands, and destroy healthy tissue. The result is a body out of balance or dis-eased.

Most cats that are not healthy have been exposed to:

- Standard commercial pet foods and artificially made treats that are sweetened or yeast-based
- Shotgun medications (the indiscriminate use of standard medications)
- Excessive vaccinations and yearly boosters—especially during surgical procedures
- Toxic cleaning products and pest control products (especially collars or monthly drug doses)
- Environmental pollution (without the benefit of regular detoxification)
- An emotionally and/or physically stressful living environment (past and present)

I believe that commercial pet food and treats account for the largest assault on cats' bodies and are the primary reason pets develop symptoms. I am not talking about food allergies here. It is my belief that the quality (or lack of good fresh quality) of the ingredient can do more harm than the ingredient itself. Many cats that previously tested positive for an allergy to a certain food are now eating it without any problems. The answer is simple—holistic animal care has reversed the symptoms of the so-called allergy. The by-products and meat, certified as unfit for human consumption, present in most commercial pet foods severely compromise the cat's ability to digest and assimilate nutrients. The artificial colors or flavors, chemical preservatives, nitrates, and rancid animal fats present in commercial pet food similarly interfere with digestion. Poorly digested matter becomes harder to eliminate, causing a back-up of old fecal material in the bowel, which further prohibits assimilation of vital nutrients. In unhealthy (or toxic) cats, ingested hair is also trapped in the bowel and stomach.

Cats often lack exercise and proper hydration. A cat fed poor-quality food loaded with chemicals and by-products will not be able to properly digest the food. This undigested matter moves into the colon, but since complete evacuation is not really possible, left-over fecal matter hardens and lines the walls of the colon. Chemicals (such as ethoxyquin, a commonly used pet food preservative that is a moisture prohibitive) dehydrate the stool, limit the lubrication necessary for a properly evacuated stool, finally producing small, hard, dry stools.

Many companies state that these stools indicate their pet food is "more digestible with less waste," but what do you think a physician would say to you if you described your own stools as small, hard lumps? Certainly, a better-quality food will produce less stool volume (generally due to less fillers and better digestibility), but it should not be caused by the lack of moisture in the stool. The colon requires ample hydration to function properly. Always provide fresh, filtered drinking water and be sure that your cat is drinking.

As old fecal material builds up inside the colon, it becomes harder and harder for the body to clean out this material on its own. This interferes with the body's ability to absorb or "ventilate" nutrients from digested matter in the colon into the bloodstream for distribution among the body's hungry cells and energy-depleted organ systems.

The next most common cause of cats' ill health is their exposure to chemicals and irritants in other, non-dietary, forms. This can be as simple as a chemical-based breath mint given as a treat, or as complicated as annual vaccination boosters. Included in this list of irritants are artificially perfumed shampoo, medicated skin treatments, flea or tick control products, household cleaning agents, and long-term medication. If you think of the body as a healthy balanced scale, and you keep adding these chemicals to one side, the scale will be tipped off-balance. But if you keep good nutrition replenished on one side and minimize the build-up of chemicals on the other, this scale stays in balance and the body stays healthy.

There are other factors that may cause a state of imbalance. Structural imbalances are often a prime underlying cause of dis-ease. Old injuries or genetic malfunctions such as rheumatoid arthritis can place stress on certain organ systems. A build-up of calcium deposits and joint or spinal inflammation may also put pressure on specific nerves involved with digestive organs, such as the stomach. This can interfere with normal stomach function, leading to improper digestion and poor assimilation of nutrients. Often, addressing the structural problems will help reverse the chronic condition. Chiropractic adjustments, massage, acupressure, and acupuncture can help you reverse your cat's symptoms.

There are other causes of a cat's imbalance. Negative emotions and a stressful environment are often overlooked. Have you ever felt butterflies in your stomach and had diarrhea due to a stressful situation? Cats who frequently experience extreme emotions (fear, nervousness, and tension) are also more likely to suffer from behavioral issues, digestive problems, and glandular imbalance. Cats experience stress due to family changes such as relocating, members leaving or dying, divorce, new births, new jobs, etc.

The pituitary, adrenal, and thyroid glands are very susceptible to hyperstimulation and exhaustion brought on by chronic emotional stress. These glands are associated with the fight-or-flight reaction to negative stimulus that is common to all living beings. Therefore, it is important to provide a safe and nurturing environment for your cat. Nutritional supplementation and remedies (especially flower essences) that re-balance the emotions are very helpful—they can often be the keys to a more complete physical healing.

When an animal's health is out of balance, waste builds up in the bloodstream and burdens eliminatory organs. Urea, the normal waste product of meat protein metabolism, is often the culprit, accounting for the large number of pets who test positive for meat allergies. The poorer the quality of meat and the more difficult it is to digest, the more waste products are produced during its digestion. As urea builds up in the body, a gout-like reaction may occur. Because it is difficult to break down, yeast can burden the liver. However, the trouble is that yeast is found in practically all commercial pet foods.

Urea or yeast toxicity manifests itself in certain symptoms, most notably:

- Known or suspected allergies to yeast, beef, pork, meat, meat by-products, or meal
- Ear infections, eye discharges, and upper respiratory problems, including asthma
- Excessive licking and chewing, resulting in bald spots and hair balls
- Prickly heat-type rashes, itchy skin, with or without hot spots, chin acne, or pustules
- Slower healing of skin problems and excessive loss of hair or coat condition
- Foul-smelling breath, flatulence, and/or stool (especially with mucus or off-colored)
- Increased fatty tumor, cyst, or cancerous tumor production
- Poor digestion and assimilation of nutrients
- Blood sugar instability, diabetes
- High levels of liver enzymes and eosinophils detected (represents a damaged liver)
- Decreased phosphates found in the urine (due to kidney disease)
- Liver, pancreatic, gall bladder, and kidney dysfunction or failure
- Weakened immune responses, especially chronic infections or cancer
- Premature aging, with or without chronic arthritic or digestive symptoms
- Neurological issues, including seizures
- Aggression and other training or behavioral problems
- Increased sensitivities to pollution, vaccinations, and chemicals in general
- Parasitic infestation, especially fleas and ticks (which feed off of skin-eliminated waste)

I have seen research which indicates that using garlic by itself is more powerful against flea and tick infestations than yeast used alone or yeast used in combination with garlic. A clean diet, which results in fewer waste products, greatly reduces the waste that must be eliminated through the skin. Excess waste is the very thing that attracts a flea or tick to the body in the first place and then feeds them. Old fecal material in the colon also attracts and feeds internal parasites such as worms.

As urea, metabolized yeast, and other excessive wastes or chemicals build up in the body and undue stress is placed upon vital organs, it is not uncommon for the body to begin experiencing system malfunctions. This vicious cycle is clearly identifiable if you know what to look for. First, the digestive system is affected, making it even harder to break down ingredients. More waste products are circulating, and fewer nutrients are available. Then the eliminatory system becomes burdened, placing undue stress upon the lymphatic and immune systems. Chronic symptoms develop, which are suppressed with medication. Once medication is stopped, the symptoms return and the cycle continues. Ultimately, there is organ and glandular malfunction, possibly leading to an early death. Frequently, the illness may seem to come out of nowhere. You might exclaim, "Yesterday she was so healthy," but this kind of breakdown does not happen overnight. It takes time for the body to become so overburdened, and there are always early warning signs that this breakdown is taking place.

Any cat suffering from poor health related to genetics, sensitivities, allergies, or toxicity can truly benefit from holistic animal care. A wholesome, toxic-free approach to diet and environment can not only prevent a symptom, it can help reverse it more quickly and effectively than the further application of chemicals.

When pets with chronic dis-ease are placed on an ongoing holistic animal care lifestyle program, the results can be miraculous. As each month passes and the body strengthens, it becomes less and less sensitive to toxins. The animal then exhibits less severe symptoms with each cycle, becoming easier to treat each time. Current acute symptoms are reversed more quickly. Cats who are healthy to begin with realize their full genetic potential. You won't know until you see the results and can compare your cat before and after holistic animal care.

Once a better diet is implemented, don't stop detoxification and supplementation immediately after the symptoms have been suppressed. If you do so, the body will become burdened again (having already shown a predisposition to this weakness) and will again react to allergens or stress. Continue supporting the immune system with a correct diet in order to prevent reoccurrence of such symptoms.

Addressing your cat's symptoms holistically is the quickest, most effective way to completely reverse an underlying condition. In those animals that have been genetically or environmentally predisposed to deeper dis-ease, holistic animal care will, in the long run, serve to minimize degenerative possibilities and maximize what curative potential there is.

Nutrition...as Nature Intended!

The primary line of defense in preventing or treating symptoms is a sound nutritional program. Your cat's natural diet should consist of fresh, high-quality ingredients that are easy to digest and assimilate. Home cooking is optimal, but might not be practical for you. Therefore, you must be very careful to seek out a quality commercial product. Become an educated label reader. Look beyond catchy terms such as "natural," "organic," "healthy," "symptom-related diet," and "human-grade quality." Ask the manufacturer directly to prove their quality and guarantee their formula.

Seek out only Grade A or B meats (human grade). Avoid the four-D meats: dead, dying, diseased, or disabled animals not fit for human consumption. Four-D meats are most commonly used in pet foods. Grain by-products also present a big problem in commercial pet products. Wheat millings, brewer's rice (leftovers from brewing), and flours are inexpensive fillers so devoid of nutritional value that they can severely compromise your cat's health. Often these grains are purchased rancid and moldy (to save money), adding to the possibility of a toxic reaction. Grade 1 or 2 grains (all human grades) should only be used, preferably whole ground, to ensure that their nutritional goodness remains intact. Go for the best quality you can afford—think of it as an insurance policy against poor health and future expenses.

Beware of "lite" diets—they may actually cause weight gain in the long run. Filler may be filling, but it is devoid of nutrients. The brain decides if there is enough nutrition available, regardless of the diet, and stores calories to ward off starvation. A properly balanced, quality diet that provides easy to assimilate nutrients will naturally bring your cat to the proper weight.

People are often concerned that changing their cat's diet will only result in digestive upsets. This is true, if you are changing from one poor-quality or chemical-based diet to another! When switching to a healthier, more natural diet, there should be no irritating ingredients to upset the balance. Often, the biggest problem during transition may be soft stool and gas, due to the fact that you probably are overfeeding your cat on the new diet. However, cats can become addicted to artificial or sweetener-based ingredients in their food. Although salt is a cat's preferred flavor enhancer, since cats normally avoid dry, rancid-smelling foods, sweeteners are added to flavor food ingredients that cats would normally avoid. Too much sugar in a cat's diet can cause pancreatic problems as well as burdening other vital organs including the liver, kidneys, adrenal and thyroid gland. Therefore, when changing your cat's diet from one filled with chemicals to a healthier variety, it is best to wean them off these addictive chemicals slowly. Add a half portion of old food to a half portion of the new diet for one week, followed by gradually increasing the amount of new food over old during the next week until the daily diet consists solely of the new diet.

One cup of a grocery store food is full of filler, almost fifty percent. When switching to a higher-quality food, there generally is less filler. Therefore, feeding the same quantities (cup for cup) will result in overfeeding and gastric upset. Your best bet is to carefully read and follow the manufacturer's specific recommendations for the food, and then watch your pet carefully for the first few weeks to see how she or he reacts.

Overfeeding often occurs when people begin cooking for their pets. I suggest that you seek out a well-researched book on natural pet care that includes home-cooked recipes.

I recommend that you don't feed your cat raw meat. Although this is now becoming more common, I have encountered many sick animals who have been fed such a diet. I believe that animals evolve to fit their environment, and since our pets have been domesticated for so long, they have evolved into processed food eaters. They have lost the ability to digest raw meat tissue, bone, hide, feathers, etc., on a regular basis.

Even with the use of digestive enzymes, I still see most pets struggling to digest raw animal tissue. Don't get me wrong here—I prefer home-cooked foods to commercially processed pet foods. The simple fact of the matter is that lightly cooking (which does not destroy all the enzymes and nutrients) helps to break down meat so that it is easier to digest. Frequently, meat has not been properly handled and can pass e. coli or parasites to the cat, leading to gastrointestinal distress.

I should emphasize that, even with the best-quality, balanced diet (using cooked or raw meats), nutritional supplementation is necessary to provide many of the nutrients now missing from our food chain. For instance, some research indicates that fifty years ago spinach had up to eighty percent more nutritional value than today! This is true (in varying degrees) for other vegetables, grains, and fruits, as well as meats from animals fed off the land. Our earth has been stripped of many naturally occurring micronutrients that used to be found in soil, and our vegetables are only as good as the soil they grow in. Years of over-farming, the use of toxic chemicals or fertilizers, and environmental pollution such as acid rain have taken their toll.

Even organic farming methods cannot guarantee that the produce will be more nutritious, as it will take approximately seventy-five years before the nutrients return to the soil.

Therefore, it is important that we supplement our animal's (and our own) diets to ensure that we receive the fundamental nutrients required. Even cat foods that are "nutritionally complete" according to AAFCO (American Association of Feed Control Officers) guidelines aren't complete according to what is truly needed for basic good health. For instance, the guidelines allow so much protein per cup of food, but that protein does not have to be *digestible*, therefore, it cannot be assimilated as protein! The same holds true for certain sources of Vitamin A or calcium, just to name a few. Therefore, proper nutrition not only includes quality, easy to digest foods, but also the appropriate supplementation to support optimum wellness, while stimulating your cat's curative potential, when needed, for symptom reversal.

The key ingredients for a healthy feline diet are:

• Fresh ingredients with no unpleasant odor (indicates rancidity)
• Whole foods such as whole-ground grains, not "flours," "mill runs," or "by-products"
• Concentrated protein sources known as "meal" (as in "lamb meal" or "beef meal") are preferred over whole meats (listed only as "lamb"). This is not to be confused with "by-product meal" (see list of ingredients to avoid)

The term "meal" simply refers to the process of removing up to eighty percent, but no less than forty-five percent, of the ingredient's natural water content, so there is more meat protein for your money (since water only adds to the ingredients' weight). The ingredients are listed on the label by weight with the heaviest ingredient first. For instance, it is deceiving to find chicken listed first when the majority of protein in the pet food is in reality coming from grains, not animal protein. This formula greatly reduces the cost of ingredients for the manufacturer, due to the actual amount of animal protein used.

Because one pound of meal is equal to approximately three pounds of whole meat, and there is an additional charge to dehydrate the meat, meal is expensive to produce. Therefore, many companies use the meat to draw you to the label, but use a cheaper ingredient for the actual protein—one that may trigger symptoms. This is true for all chicken, turkey, rabbit, fish, and other animal protein sources used in commercial pet foods.

Look for the following ingredients on your pet food label:

- Identifiable, digestible animal protein or fat sources such as beef, beef meal, lamb, lamb meal, lamb fat, chicken, chicken meal or chicken fats, turkey, ostrich, etc., not vague terms like "meats," "mammal," or "animal fats"

- USDA Grade A or B animal protein sources, preferably raised without growth hormones or recently given antibiotics

- USDA Grade 1 or 2 whole grains preferably free of chemical pesticides or herbicides. Organic grains are not cost-effective in commercial pet foods. If the label on the food you are feeding your pet says "organic," demand written certification. However, "pesticide-free" is available, or "washed" grains are possible. For home cooking, go for the best ingredients you can afford!

- Balanced, combined ingredients of proteins and grain sources seem to suit most pets better than a single ingredient, contrary to popular belief.

- Vegetable and fruit fiber should be present (for example, carrots and apples) for proper digestion, natural flavoring, and trace nutrients. Fiber in general is very important to proper elimination. Moreover, fiber (additionally provided in whole grains) might as well be full of vital nutrients.

- Quality sources of fat and fatty acids (necessary for energy and good coats) such as vegetable or fish oils should be used, in addition to animal fats. Unlike dogs, who do not digest animal fats well, cats need the energy only found in sufficient quantities in animal fats. These animal fats must be from a high-quality, fresh source.

- Ample levels of Taurine, an amino acid that is essential for cats, are needed to trigger several biochemical processes. Taurine aids in the deactivation of toxins in the liver and helps maintain proper heart rhythm. Deficient levels of Taurine can lead to neurological problems including seizures, and degeneration of the retina, eventually leading to blindness. Cats cannot synthesize Taurine, so pet food companies must now supplement feline formulas with Taurine. If it is suspected that a cat is not assimilating Taurine properly, additional supplementation with fifty mg. to one hundred mg. of Taurine (available at natural pet food stores) or two to four tablespoons of diced clams per day may trigger a curative response.

- Priced appropriately, remember that you do generally get what you pay for! Suppose you pay $8.00 for a 20-pound bag of food, and the cost of making and marketing the food is as follows: paper bag costs 85 cents, shipping 50 cents, advertising and handling 75 cents. This pricing will yield a $1.00 profit for the manufacturer, $1.25 profit for the wholesaler, and a $1.50 profit for the retailer. How much do you think the manufacturer actually spends on the ingredients?

- Take into consideration how much of the cheaper food you will need to sustain your cat. Often, the cheaper foods will prove to be more expensive, due to the fact that you have to use so much more food than you would with a better-quality diet, which contains less filler.

- Product should be fresh when purchased. If you bought fresh-baked bread, it would still be wonderful to eat the next day, but would you still be eating it two weeks later? Be sure to check the date the food was packed. Never use food (especially naturally preserved diets) that is older than six months, unless it is packaged in a completely sealed, airtight, barrier bag. Stale food has not only lost its flavor, but also most of its nutritional value through oxidation.

These are ingredients to avoid in a healthy diet:

- Chemical preservatives: Ethoxyquin, BHA and/or BHT, Propylene Glycol, Nitrates
- Artificial flavors or colors

- Foul-smelling ingredients must be avoided. If the food smells like traditional pet food (you know that smell, even in fresh bags it smells rancid) throw it out.

- Greasy food, that leaves smelly oil on the bag or a sheen on canned formulas, indicates that it is high in animal fats or tallow (rendered carcasses and recycled cooking grease from restaurants). These are difficult to digest and are most often rancid prior to manufacturing. This accounts for that rancid "pet food" smell, even in "fresh" bags.

- Animal by-products such as "beef by-product," "lamb by-product," "chicken by-product" (a mixture of the *whole carcass* including feces, cancerous tumors, hide, hooves, beaks, feathers, and fur). Also avoid their mysterious cousins—"meat" or "meat by-products" (a mixture of whatever mammals, including road kill, rats and dogs and other cats ground up together), "fish by-product," and "poultry by-products" (a mixture of whatever feathered animals ground together, including pigeons).

- Grain by-products such as "mill runs," "flours," "middlings," "husks," and "parts" should be avoided at all costs. Not only have they had all their nutritionally rich parts already removed, they may irritate the digestive and eliminatory tracts. These grain by-products are cheap fillers and used as an additional protein source (although they cannot be digested and therefore cannot be assimilated) to increase the finished product's weight and mass.

- Fillers such as powdered "cellulose," or "cellulose fiber" can include recycled newspaper, sawdust, and cardboard. "Plant cellulose" usually means ground peanut hulls, which are very damaging to sensitive colon tissues. Beet pulp or grain by-products have no nutritional value, but do add bulk and weight to the finished product.

- Yeast is a cheap source of B Vitamins, amino acids, and some nutrients. It also adds natural flavor and color. It is touted for flea control and a shiny coat, but yeast can contribute to symptoms by burdening the liver and interfering with proper digestion.

- Sugar is added to most commercial diets and treats. It is labeled as "sucrose," "beet pulp," "molasses," "cane syrup," "fruit solids," and, of course, "sugar." It is a very cheap and heavy filler, which is addictive for cats. Additional sugar in the diet is the primary trigger of weight problems, diabetic conditions, and behavioral problems in pets today.
- Salt is added to enhance flavor and to encourage cats to drink more water. Salt is *considered a preventative* to Feline Urological Syndrome (F.U.S.), but can lead to heart problems or hypertension, digestive problems, stress on the urinary tract, and respiratory weakness.

I recommend supplementing the food you feed your cat (no matter how good it is) with a well-balanced vitamin and mineral supplement. Seek out a high-quality, high-potency, daily multiple. Food-source supplements are excellent choices for the general maintenance of healthy cats, but they are not potent enough to prevent or reverse significant disease in a genetically compromised or chronically ill pet. Be sure that you provide at least the minimum requirements of vital nutrients, because, for whatever reason, your cat might not be able to assimilate her food completely. It is additional insurance. I recommend these nutrients daily for most adult cats:

- Vitamin A (2,500 mg.) for a strong immune system, eyes, tissue repairs; prevents tissue (weight) loss during illness
- Beta Carotene (1,500 mg.) to support Vitamin A assimilation
- Vitamin B1 (25 mg.) for energy and emotional well-being
- Vitamin B2 (25 mg.) necessary for fat and carbohydrate metabolism, especially to promote curative response
- Vitamin B6 (25 mg.) red blood cell production and protein metabolism; natural diuretic, relieves edema
- Vitamin B12 (25 mcg.) aids in calcium absorption; is anti-inflammatory; prevents anemia common to cats
- Niacin (25 mg.) promotes healthy skin and nerves; supports digestion; helps prevent feline acne

- Pantothenic Acid (25 mg.) is an anti-oxidant vital to adrenal activity; developing antibodies and reducing toxins
- Folic Acid (100 mcg.) necessary for DNA; enzyme efficiency, and blood; reduces problems of malabsorbtion
- Choline (25 mg.) vital neurotransmitter; works with Inositol to emulsify fats; supports liver function
- Inositol (25 mg.) lowers fatty deposits in the liver; controls cholesterol and benefits the diabetic cat
- PABA (25 mg.) protects skin from sun-related cancer; supports coat color; may reduce skin growths
- Biotin (25 mcg.) aids metabolism of fatty acids and amino acids; makes antibodies; promotes good coat condition
- Vitamin C (100 mg.) repairs connective tissue; builds resistance to cancer, allergies, F.U.S., autoimmune disorder
- Vitamin D (100 I.U.) with Vitamin A helps cat utilize calcium and phosphorus; essential for healthy thyroid
- Vitamin E (25 I.U.) is an exceptional antioxidant, triggers tissue repair; oxygenates the tissues
- Calcium (15 mg.) needed for strong bones and teeth; reduces muscular stress; enhances colon condition to pass fur
- Phosphorus (5 mg.) supports structure, oxygen to the brain, maintains pH, reduces muscular fatigue
- Magnesium (1.75 mg.) critical for bones, nerve, and muscle function; prevents and reverses stone formation
- Potassium (2.5 mg.) supports electrolyte and pH balance, neurotransmitter; vital to cardiovascular health
- Iron (4.5 mg.) combines with proteins to form red blood cells
- Manganese (1.5 mg.) nourishes the brain, nerves; supports SOD/antioxidant activity, eliminates pain
- Zinc (4 mg.) co-enzyme of SOD—protects against free radicals which may promote cancer and other disease
- Iodine (38 mcg.) vital to proper thyroid function and proper metabolism for tissue development and repairs
- Copper (75 mcg.) for inflammatory response, bone mineralization, coat color; necessary for protein metabolism
- Glutamic Acid (6 mg.) supports nerve health; metabolizes fats and sugars; detoxifies ammonia in the brain

• Selenium and Chromium (6 mcg. each) stimulate the immune system and slow down the aging process

To introduce a dietary change, and to kick off a successful program for prevention or rehabilitation, begin by imposing a twenty-four hour period of fasting. Many people associate fasting with starving their cat. This couldn't be further from the truth—fasting can save your cat's life!

Fasting encourages the body to detoxify and re-balance. The fasting methods I suggest are safe and gentle. The pleading, begging look your cat might give you at dinnertime may bother you the most. Twenty-five percent of that look may be hunger-related, but the other seventy-five percent is definitely control-related. Pets, particularly cats, are experts at controlling their masters.

To avoid that pleading look while your cat is fasting, do something fun with your cat at his usual dinnertime. Bring home a new toy (but don't do it out of guilt!) or take your friend out for a fifteen-minute romp in the fresh air. These activities will occupy you and your cat's thoughts and will provide exercise. If you still feel guilty, just remind yourself that they are *begging for their life.*

Anyone who has tried to clean a counter with a dirty sponge knows that a clean sponge is more effective. During a fast, old fecal material will be expelled from the colon while vital eliminatory organs, such as the kidneys and liver, are given a break from processing daily waste, thus allowing for a deeper elimination of backed-up toxins. This results in improved digestive and eliminatory systems. Good processing is necessary for the intake of both nutrients and therapeutic substances (which will help strengthen the immune system and build resistance to sensitivities). The reduction of toxins in the body also improves the overall condition of your cat, and sometimes will help reverse most symptoms. It is common, following a short fast and detoxification that the more obvious symptoms immediately begin to improve.

Usually within the first six to eight weeks after detoxification, you will see a reversal of symptoms. I have observed that seventy-five percent of cats that have been detoxed and given a better diet along with basic nutritional support will be happier and healthier. In the remaining twenty-five percent of cases, including those with chronic debilitating dis-ease, the judicious use of homeopathic, herbal, and nutritional supplementation in a *continuing* course of treatment will definitely strengthen each animal's constitution and reduce or eventually eliminate their condition. With chronic cases, it can often take several weeks, even a year, to build up the body enough to eliminate the symptoms completely.

Simply suppressing symptoms pharmaceutically is not only frustrating but may lead to a premature death. Year after year toxins attacking a body—barely protected by a struggling immune system—will only serve to weaken the body further. A sound nutritional program supported with ongoing detoxification, proper supplementation, and re-balancing with homeopathic remedies or herbs, while avoiding (or at least limiting) vaccination boosters, chemicals, and drugs, is the best way to strengthen your cat's immune system and prevent or reverse poor health.

The first step to take now towards establishing a successful holistic animal care program is proper detoxification. Detoxification prepares the body to digest and assimilate nutrients that are vital to heal and strengthen your cat. No matter what wonderful new products you feed your cat, if your pet cannot properly utilize a product's nutritive or therapeutic properties, the end results will probably be disappointing. In fact, without proper detoxification, you are severely limiting the body's overall curative potential.

There are gentle and effective ways to stimulate the body's eliminatory systems (the colon, kidneys, liver, lungs, skin, and lymph system) to remove waste on a deeper level than what is required for daily maintenance. By utilizing these methods, you help your cat prevent symptoms from occurring, and you will also help your cat to reverse and possibly completely eliminate dis-ease.

Detoxification and Fasting

DETOXIFICATION THROUGH FASTING

Fasting is the method many people have used to detoxify their pets' bodies. Fasting is much more than simply withholding food. It gently re-balances the body. Always check with your veterinarian first before you start a fast, to be certain that there are no medical reasons such a program is not wise at this time. Possibly you are treating your cat for feline leukemia and must maintain their appetite and give drugs with feeding, or perhaps your veterinarian feels that your cat is too weak to fast, due to a recent bout of minor infections. (In fact, these are perfect times to fast.)

Although I have successfully fasted many animals in such circumstances, it is always wise to rely on the advice of a trusted veterinarian, especially if you have one who encourages you in your endeavors to support your cat with a holistic lifestyle.

There are two methods of detoxification I recommend.

STANDARD FAST

The standard method is for cats who have acute or chronic symptoms, but who are otherwise in good health. Age makes no difference. I have seen twenty-two-year-old cats as well as sick one-week-old kittens respond to this standard fast. It is pretty straightforward, assuming that your cat is fairly healthy to begin with, but you may still have to adjust the process according to your cat's specific needs.

Day One
- Feed breakfast as you normally would on the morning you are to begin the fast. Simply eliminate the evening meal.
- Be sure to provide plenty of fresh drinking water.

- Provide fun-filled activity in fresh air and sunshine twice during the day of fasting followed by a damp terry cloth rubdown.
- Be sure not to overtire or stress your pet.

Day Two—Breaking the Fast
Breaking the fast is as important as the fast itself.

- After 24 hours of fasting you'll feed your cat one-half her normal quantity of breakfast. Cooked oatmeal with tuna water or natural baby food is a good choice for breaking the fast.
- Again provide exercise in the fresh air and sunshine twice during the day, followed by a damp terry cloth rubdown.
- Remember to give your cat plenty of water and be sure not to overtire or stress your pet. If you do, you will take energy away from the curative process.
- For dinner, simply return to the normal quantity (and hopefully, better quality) of food.

To make this process really special, break the fast with *cooked oatmeal* (excellent for absorbing impurities in the digestive tract) and tuna water instead of the regular diet, again at about one-half the normal quantity. A teaspoon of *raw honey*, encapsulated *garlic oil* (raw garlic can be too harsh at this point) and some type of *fresh green extract* such as *barley grass* or *spirulina* can be very soothing and cleansing to the digestive system after fasting. For some very finicky cats dilute a teaspoon of liquid chlorophyll in two tablespoons of tuna water, and, using a feeding syringe give the liquid in small, frequent doses. Wrap your cat in a towel when feeding from a syringe to calm them and protect you from claws. Supplements can also be added back into the diet following the fast.

This is a good fasting protocol to follow at the first sign of dis-ease, to help stimulate a curative response and well-being. I do not recommend fasting a cat on a regular basis since they require a frequent intake of calories and can become too stressed when fasted too often. I prefer to fast my cats when they are herbally treated twice a year for parasite prevention. I detoxify my cats homeopathically on a weekly basis and provide herbs for general cleansing and healthy functioning of the digestive tract.

You will quickly find what type of fasting suits you and your cat's needs. Remember that exercise is very important at all times to help move toxins out of the body by further stimulating the eliminatory organs. The terry cloth rubdown helps to stimulate the skin and to aid it while it continues to process waste from the body's detoxification.

If an odor is present during fasting, add three tablespoons baking soda to one quart of warm, purified water, apply the solution to the towel, and rub your cat's body with the towel. Dry your cat's body with a clean, dry towel. The baking soda will help to neutralize the odor and balance the skin's pH, reducing itching. Avoid using tap water, as it contains chlorine, which will be absorbed into the skin. Chlorine is very counterproductive to a successful detoxification. It is a known skin irritant and will increase itching. If tap water is the only available water, boil it for fifteen minutes to help evaporate the chlorine. Be sure to let the boiled tap water cool down before using. A lemon cut up and boiled in the water for twenty minutes and then strained, makes a wonderful deodorizer and acts as a disinfectant as well.

For cats with special needs, cutting back twenty-five to fifty percent of their standard meal, while adding nutritional supplements, herbal extracts, and vegetable and fruit juices, will increase elimination, without upsetting their metabolism.

SUPPORTIVE PHYTOCHEMICALS

Listed below are the best detoxifying herbs, vegetables, and fruits that are gentle enough to use during fasting.

- *Milk Thistle* is good for liver cleansing and support.
- *Dandelion* is an effective blood purifier and general organ cleanser. Helps stabilize appetite.
- *Burdock Root* helps remove catabolic waste from cellular activity.
- *Slippery Elm* is very soothing to inflamed colon tissues and helps settle the stomach and eliminate furballs.
- *Yucca*, a natural anti-inflammatory, supports circulation, and reduces discomfort. Soothes the digestive tract.
- *Garlic*, a potent anti-bacterial, anti-viral, anti-fungal, and anti-parasitic agent, protects cats from heartworm.
- *Kombu* alkalizes the body and purifies the blood of fats.
- *Spirulina* is high in chlorophyll and aids enzyme production and digestion. Helps stimulate appetite during illness.
- *Carrots* are trace mineral-rich and high in vitamins. They alkalize the body and are flavorful. Try carrot slivers for treats.
- *Beets* provides several supportive nutrients, fiber, and flavor.
- *Parsnips* provide wonderful support for detoxifying the kidneys.
- *Spinach* is an excellent source of nutrients and trace minerals.
- *Celery* is trace mineral-rich, and high in vitamins. It alkalizes the body and is flavorful. Cats love to crunch raw celery!
- *Parsley* is trace mineral-rich, oxygenating to the blood, and helps reduce odors.
- *Ginger* can help the digestive system, reduce gas, and aid hypertension.
- *Apples* provide needed energy while supporting detoxification.
- *Cranberries* are very high in Vitamin C and help flush urinary tract waste.
- *Papaya* rebalances the body, aids digestion, and helps flush waste.

Avoid harsh or highly acidic vegetables like tomatoes and onions, or difficult-to-digest ingredients like cabbage. Also avoid the use of harsh fibers such as psyllium, which can further irritate and damage sensitive intestinal tissues. Although psyllium does produce bulk and encourages elimination, its negative side effects, when used alone, outweigh its benefits during detoxification.

HOMEOPATHIC DETOXIFICATION

To encourage elimination further, no matter what fasting protocol you choose, it is best to combine fasting with homeopathic detoxification. If you decide not to fast your cat or your cat cannot be fasted for medical reasons, homeopathic detoxification works by itself and is safe for all animals. Its only drawback is that it can take almost twice as long to achieve the end result as when it is combined with fasting. On the other hand, fasting alone can take even longer to work than homeopathic detoxification alone, so opt for homeopathy if you need to choose one over the other.

One or several individual remedies may be chosen, based on your individual cat's needs. Or you may find that one of the many combination products available works just as well.

For detoxification, use the lower potencies, Xs to low Cs. Homeopathic detoxification should be used daily for no less than two weeks, preferably six to eight weeks. Give one daily dose at bedtime for most cases, or one dose upon rising and again at bedtime for more chronic cases. Do not give remedies within thirty minutes of feeding or giving strong herbs.

When beginning a homeopathic remedy, I recommend building up its action in the body through frequent dosing. You cannot overdose your pet. Give one dose orally, according to the manufacturer's recommendations, every fifteen minutes for the first hour, then once or twice daily, and any other time your cat needs additional detoxification.

After the initial detoxification process, a maintenance program can be initiated on a weekly basis. Maintenance means a single weekly dose at bedtime to help process current waste build-up, stimulate proper kidney and liver functions, and support general good health. It does not mean that homeopathic detoxification should be used in lieu of proper feeding, supplementation, and care. It acts to support digestion and elimination. See "Holistic Cat Care," for specific solutions and remedy suggestions.

Arsenicum and *Nux Vomica* are often the homeopaths' first remedies of choice to establish equilibrium of biological functions and to counteract many chronic effects. They balance the overall body during detoxification. They help to counteract nausea, irritability, digestive disturbances, and liver congestion sometimes associated with the detoxification process. In my opinion, they should always be included in a detoxification program, regardless of what other remedies are chosen. The best homeopathic combinations for detoxification on the market today include these two remedies. I have even often reversed many acute toxic reactions (including pesticide poisonings) with the use of *Arsenicum* and *Nux Vomica* alone. When in doubt, this is a sound combination to try.

HELPFUL HINTS TO AID GENERAL DETOXIFICATION AND THE CURATIVE PROCESS

- *Provide plenty of pure water.* Water is needed to facilitate the flushing of wastes. Avoid using tap water containing chlorine and chemicals (which may be too harsh for the kidneys), or distilled water (which may accelerate the detoxification). Be sure that your cat's drinking water is always free of metals and sediments.
- *Groom daily* to help brush away toxins being eliminated through the skin. Longhaired cats need grooming to circulate fresh air to the skin. Grooming stimulates blood circulation, further

aiding elimination and the removal of old, dead skin, and stimulating the growth of new, healthier coats. Wipe away any ear, eye, penile, vaginal, or anal discharges to avoid infections.

- *Provide daily exercise in fresh air and sunshine* to encourage circulation and respiration, which supports the removal of deeper toxins. This also improves your cat's attitude, and thereby her healing. If your cat lives indoors, provide a screened area with cat trees or solid wood furniture covered with carpet and rope for your cat to climb.

- *Respect your cat's quiet times and needs* even if they seem to be withdrawing from the family. It is normal for cats going through detoxification to sleep more, refuse to eat a meal or two (continuing the fasting process on their own when needed), become irritable or nervous, and seek out warmer or cooler areas. Do not force feed during this time.

- *Avoid the use of all chemicals and drugs* that are not absolutely necessary for sustaining life. Drugs will interfere with the detoxification process and may be even more harmful to your cat during this time. As the curative process moves deeper into the constitution, the body may react even more than usual to these substances, possibly causing a reaction.

- *Avoid giving a vaccine booster* within six weeks prior to, or after, this type of detoxification. Shortly after a vaccination, it will be more difficult for the body to detoxify. If detoxification is completed before a vaccination, the body may react more strongly to the vaccination. Cats often get sick regardless.

- *Address symptom aggravations gently* through the use of nutritional supplementation, homeopathy, flower essences, or herbs. This will allow the cleansing process to continue, while keeping the symptoms subdued.

- *Keep track of your cat's progress* to help you understand the process they are actually going through. If you jot down a few notes each day, you will be less likely to be afraid, and scare yourself into thinking that it has been "days" since your cat last ate, when in fact it might have only been two meals.

If a discharge started three days age and was clear but has turned yellow, you will need to add natural antibiotics such as garlic or Echinacea to fight off any possible infections. Then you will want to keep track of how many days the discharge remains yellow, or how quickly it responds to the garlic or Echinacea. You may want to seek other support if necessary. On the other hand, if you noted that the discharge took two weeks to clear up and then returned in three weeks, but only took four days to clear up this second time, and did not return for two months the third time, then you will begin to see a pattern which indicates you are on the right track!

Each time the body experiences a curative response which has been supported rather than suppressed, it gets stronger and the symptoms return less frequently and less aggressively until, eventually, the symptoms are eliminated (reversed) completely.

WHAT TO EXPECT DURING DETOXIFICATION AND RE-BALANCING

Detoxification is the process of dumping waste. Therefore, waste will present itself during the process. This includes, but is not limited to, the aggravation of the very symptoms you are trying to address by starting this cleansing process. This is a good sign! Referred to as a *curative response*, it is a clear indication that the body has been stimulated into cleansing by whatever detoxification protocol you are following. When this response occurs, many people become frightened and run to their veterinarian to get a drug to suppress these symptoms. This is the worse thing that can be done at this time.

It is vital that these symptoms be supported rather than suppressed at this time. If you choose to suppress these symptoms with holistic animal care or drugs, you will force the underlying imbalance even deeper. Chemicals and medications at this point, especially steroids and antibiotics, will severely burden the body. At the very least, you will have prematurely terminated the cleansing process through fear. But realize that this means that you and your pet will eventually have to go through the process once more if you can ever hope for true healing. It is best to address the symptoms gently and naturally while continuing the detoxification process. Many things can be done to minimize the curative response without suppressing the cleansing and strengthening process.

Please note that aggravations *do not* have to occur for the body to be properly detoxifying. It is more common for the process to happen relatively easily for most pets, regardless of their previous conditions!

It should be noted that cats who seemed to be in balance and healthy prior to detoxification can exhibit the worst symptoms during detoxification. This response can be caused by an imbalance *years ago* that was suppressed *back then*. You must be aware of your own pet's individual process and support that, no matter what preconceived notions you may have had regarding what the process *should be* like.

ADDRESSING COMMON CURATIVE RESPONSES

Curative responses are a natural part of the cleansing process. It is vital to the ongoing strengthening of the body *to support these symptoms rather than suppress them*. The safest, most effective way to support symptom aggravations is through the gentle modalities of nutritional supplements, homeopathy, flower essences, and herbs. Please, do not forget the power of love, play, and contact. Spend time nurturing your pet. It will certainly help minimize any stress they may be experiencing during the curative process.

Holistic Cat Care

Now that you are giving your cat a sound foundation—supported by love, behavioral guidance, daily exercise/play, proper nutrition with supplementation, and regular detoxification—you might want to explore how to prevent or reverse genetic and chronic dis-ease. If your cat has an imbalance manifesting as a particular symptom, natural remedies can help. Herbs and homeopathy are wonderful tools to support the immune system and the curative process for both acute (sudden) or chronic (long-term) illness. Proper examination and quick response to changes can turn around a serious problem before it has a chance to become a chronic symptom.

TEN-POINT HEALTH CHECKLIST

I have prepared a ten-point health checklist so that you can quickly identify and address any weakness or imbalance when it occurs in your cat. Always have this information available the next time you visit your veterinarian, as it will help them assess the situation correctly.

1. *Nutrition*—What type of food do you feed your cat? How often do you feed your cat? Is the diet well-balanced? Bring in the label if needed. Have your cat's eating habits recently changed? Does your pet seem satisfied, or is he always hungry? Has your cat's diet changed recently? Has her food become rancid, due to age or heat? Have you introduced any new supplements, treats, chewable toys, or food ingredients that may be creating the problem?

2. *Digestion*—Does your cat have daily bowel movements? Is flatulence a problem, and when does it occur? Has the smell, volume, color, or consistency of your cat's stool changed recently?

Major signs of illness can include vomiting, diarrhea, or constipation for more than twenty-four hours. Noting such changes in stool and pursuing a clinical diagnosis can quickly identify pancreatic imbalance (fatty, discolored stool) and parasitic infestations (rice or string-like bodies within the stool). These imbalances are then much easier to reverse, before they develop into more serious conditions, such as diabetes or irritable bowel syndrome.

3. *Urination*—Do you allow free access to a potty area, or do you impose potty times around your own schedule? Have you recently changed the potty arrangement? Does your cat refuse to use the same litter or potty area as before? Has your cat's daily intake of water changed? Is her urination painful? Is his urine scant or bloody? Is there a metallic or sweet odor to it? Has your cat recently become incontinent?

4. *Skin and Coat Condition*—Has there been a change in your cat's sheen or general coat condition? Are there dry flakes, dull or greasy coat, hot spots, acne, or pimples? Have you noticed excessive shedding, hair loss, scratching, licking, fur pulling, etc.? Coat and skin condition can be a primary source of health-related observation, especially for symptoms involving the liver or kidneys. Toxic waste will often be eliminated through the skin if these organs are not kept in peak condition.

5. *Ears* can become inflamed or have a waxy discharge as the first signs of immune imbalance or toxicity. Have you seen pests, such as mites (small dark specks like pepper), for months prior to the immune system taking a serious dive? Allergies, yeast, or bacterial infections will often first manifest themselves in the ears. Are your pet's symptoms related to allergy seasons or weather changes?

6. *Eyes and Nose* may often become inflamed along with the ears. Irritated eyes can create blocked tear ducts, manifesting nasal discharge and respiratory difficulties. Have the infected eyes quickly become matted and painful? Is the discharge chronic? Or seasonally related? Red, swollen eyes are symptomatic of improper liver function and detoxification, while nasal problems can be related to viral infection. Genetic conditions, such as turned-in lashes, can be addressed early on before they cause permanent damage and even blindness.

7. *Nervous System, Bones, Joints, and Muscles*—Has your pet recently shown signs of confusion, lethargy, or uncontrollable shaking? Difficulty drinking or eating? Any rapid weight changes? Has her gait or movement, especially getting up or down, changed? Is there noticeable pain or limping? Restless sleep or exhaustion? Is there any body odor or fever present? A cat's normal temperature is 100° to 102°. Breeds who are more energetic, such as Siamese, may have slightly higher normal readings, up to 102.2°. Use a digital thermometer for one minute to take the temperature.

8. *Respiratory and Cardiac*—Has your cat's breathing changed? Can she play as long as she used to before becoming winded? Has he developed a cough or wheezing, with no evidence of hairballs? Has his resting pulse rate or breathing patterns changed?

   Normal Heart Rate/Pulse: 100 to 140 beats per minute. Taken inside the thigh on the femoral artery.

9. *Emotional and Behavioral*—Has your cat recently become withdrawn, fearful, nervous, or aggressive? Has she become more destructive; chewing on herself, the furniture, or the walls? Has she suddenly begun soiling in the house? There can often be a physical problem behind these behavioral issues—just as stress can lead to health problems. Have you or your family recently gone through a divorce, moving, death (of a person or another pet), or other stressful events?

   Your cats will surely suffer the increased stress in their environment, much the way humans do. Often, they suffer more. All they are capable of understanding is that there is a problem. They can't fathom the cause of the change, or that it may soon be resolved—they just worry about it and the fact that you, as the center of their universe, are now different in a negative way.

10. *Environment*—Have you recently sprayed the yard for weeds or have you applied chemical pesticides in the house, yard, or even directly to your cat? Is your cat wearing a chemically based flea/tick collar? Are there any other poisons, radiator fluid, or toxic plants, such as poinsettias, available to your cat

to chew on or ingest in some way? Have you installed new floor covering that might be seeping formaldehyde, or other toxins that your cat is directly exposed to? Has the quality of your cat's drinking water or diet changed? Has your cat been given a new medication or recent vaccination?

All of these factors can trigger a toxic reaction, weaken the immune system, or cause an organ failure. With ninety percent of pets' health problems today created by the toxic environment, it is vital that you become aware of what it is exactly that your cat is exposed to, or ingesting.

USING HOLISTIC ANIMAL CARE SUCCESSFULLY

The key to a successful Holistic Animal Care Lifestyle is selecting the appropriate tools and correctly applying them. Be sure to seek out high-quality products *and follow the manufacturer's recommendations*. Not all nutritional or herbal products are created the same—with such varying potencies, I would be remiss to make dosage recommendations, therefore, I will focus on the proper ingredients and encourage you to educate yourself about the available products.

Remember, it can take three to six weeks for detoxification and increased assimilation of nutrients to begin establishing the necessary foundation for a successful curative process and symptom reversal. During this time old cells are being replaced with the newer, healthier cells, which will bring change to the overall condition.

Therefore, it is best to allow the body some time to respond on its own before adding too many other ingredients to the mix. Provide a high-quality multiple vitamin and mineral supplement with basic herbal or homeopathic support for the first month or two, until you better understand the specific underlying imbalance. Remember that close to eight out of ten pets successfully reverse their conditions with this alone. Additional supplements or medications may overwhelm the body with ingredients it doesn't need and interfere with the body's natural curative process. Explore each product available to see what they specifically recommend in your situation. Be sure to read ingredient labels carefully, and follow all instructions listed on any products you choose to use on your animals.

Homeopathy is safe to use in addition to herbs or medications, although drugs may interfere with a remedy's potential to trigger the curative process. Utilize homeopathy to its fullest potential by following a few simple suggestions, as it is very helpful in reducing acute flare-ups and supports symptom reversal on a deeper level than herbs or supplements alone. This can often be the key to reversing a deeper acute or chronic weakness. Although a lot of emphasis is placed on potencies, I have found many to be successful in a wide range of potencies, so today I'm more inclined to support getting what is available to you regardless if it is a 6X not a 3C. For the majority of acute reactions, even if due to chronic conditions, utilizing the lower potencies will effect change. These potencies range anywhere from 3X to 30C. For long-term reversal of a specific disorder, utilizing the higher 200C potency will be effective, once lower potencies have brought the acute reaction under control. High potencies, such as Ms, should be used under professional guidance. By giving the body a boost with homeopathic remedies, other supplements act more quickly and effectively.

When beginning a homeopathic remedy, I recommend building up its action in the body through frequent dosing. You can not overdose your pet. Give one dose orally, according to the manufacturer's recommendations, every fifteen minutes for the first hour, then every hour until there is relief. To maintain relief, dose a minimum of twice daily for an additional week or two. More frequent dosing can occur as needed. Resume this or any another appropriate remedy whenever the symptom presents itself and follow this schedule until there is complete reversal. Long-term maintenance is also possible through a weekly dose of the most beneficial remedy.

I prefer liquid remedies because they are easier to give. If the dropper touches your hands or your pet, rinse it off before returning to the bottle. Most remedies come in sugar pellets (use as is) or tablets (crush inside a piece of paper first for best application). To avoid contamination and a reduction in efficacy, always allow at least fifteen minutes apart from food or strong extracts when giving homeopathic remedies and do not handle remedies with your bare hands. Rather, use the cap or a clean piece of paper to administer the dose.

EARS, EYES, AND RESPIRATORY SYSTEM

Ear Problems can be the first sign of dis-ease, so it is important that you carefully check and clean the ears often. Early detection of parasitic infestation or bacterial and yeast infection can help prevent the spread of dis-ease into the sensitive middle and inner ear. A healthy ear should be free of smell, discharge, or oily debris, and have clear skin tone with no irritation or discomfort.

Symptoms commonly occur in toxic or allergy-sensitive cats. Many breeds are genetically prone to ear problems.

The liver, a primary organ often affected by allergens or toxins, is considered "in relation" to the ears and eyes. As the liver becomes burdened, the ears begin to exhibit symptoms associated with allergy problems and become more prone to irritation from grasses, pollen, and molds, as well as from foods and chemicals.

In addition, symptoms often occur from trapped objects. Foxtails and other foreign bodies can become lodged in the ear, triggering irritation and discharge. Always check first to see if you can find anything in your cat's ears and remove it prior to treatment. If needed, seek proper removal by a veterinarian.

Ears can be effectively cleaned with a home-made solution of two ounces purified or distilled water, one teaspoon *Witch Hazel*, one teaspoon *white vinegar*, and six drops of *Calendula Extract*. Add an additional six drops of *Golden Seal Extract* if infection is suspected. Use a cotton ball to squeeze a little of this solution into the ear, rubbing the outer base of the ear and massaging the solution into any debris that needs to be removed. You may hear a slight suction noise inside the ear. Allow your cat to shake out her ears, then wipe out the rest of the debris and fluid with a soft tissue wrapped around your finger. Do not insert anything down into the inner ear. Rather, let the tissue absorb any impurities. Follow cleanings with a light application of *Calendula Extract*, *Aloe Gel*, or *Vitamin E*. Use *Hypericum Cream* around the earflap and opening if pain is present.

Be careful not to use heavy oil-based ingredients or vegetable oils, unless you want to dissolve a foreign body or kill ear mites. Although these products may seem to condition the ear and reduce irritation, the oil may nurture a bacterial or yeast infection by providing a warm, moist, oxygen-free environment.

To dissolve a suspected foreign body which is not creating severe pain or bleeding, warm up two tablespoons of garlic-flavored cooking oil (to help discourage bacterial growth), or use soybean oil to which you have added a capsule of *Garlic Extract* with six drops each of *Golden Seal* and *Mullein Extract*, and 200 IUs of *Vitamin E*.

Apply with a dropper, spoon, or cotton ball, dripping it down into the ear. Allow it to remain there for as long as your cat will tolerate it. Finish by massaging the base of the ear to further loosen the object before flushing the ear out with the cleaning solution. Repeat several times per day until the object is removed, usually within a day or two. This will dissolve hardened debris as well as many plant particles. Never force fluid into the ear with pressure, or you may drive the object further in, making it harder to remove safely.

If the ear seems more irritated, begins to bleed profusely, becomes unbearably painful, or develops a severe discharge, or isn't responsive to home treatment within a few days, seek out veterinarian care immediately. Do not take ear problems lightly, as chronic inflammation and infections can lead to permanent damage, resulting in hearing loss. Reliance on chemically based medicated ear washes or drops can also permanently damage the sensitive tissues of the ear, resulting in increased production of oily discharge.

Grapefruit Extract eardrops can also be applied after cleaning to fight bacterial and yeast infections. *Mullein* and *Garlic Oil* eardrops are also excellent for irritated and infected ears.

Avoid alcohol-based products, which can irritate the ears further. If you suspect water is trapped in the ear canal, a few drops of pure alcohol can dry up the water residue. Don't worry about the alcohol found in any herbal extracts you might be using—only insignificant amounts of alcohol remain in the final dilution. Unless your cat is sensitive to alcohol, avoid glycerin-based herbal extracts—I have found them to be therapeutically less potent than their alcohol-based cousins.

Ear Mites or Otodectes are tiny white spider-like pests, practically impossible to see with the naked eye. They leave a trail of digested blood and debris in the ear resembling finely ground pepper. A gritty discharge results. Chronic infestation can result in hearing loss. (See Immune System Dysfunction.)

To dissolve a suspected infestation (which may not create severe pain or bleeding), warm up natural ear oil and apply as directed for removal of foreign objects. Allow it to set for as long as your cat will tolerate, at least one-half hour to dissolve any debris. Then flush the ear out with a cleaning solution. Repeat several times per day until all the mites are removed, and symptoms are reversed, usually within a day or two.

Eye Problems are almost always involved in toxicity or sensitivities, often accompanying ear symptoms. Be sure to check your cat's eyes daily, and wipe away any matter present. Always address eye problems quickly, as chronic irritation or infection can permanently damage the eye, possibly leading to cataracts, corneal ulceration, and even blindness.

To clean away slight discharge, use a warm, damp cotton cloth. Always use distilled water and wipe in the direction of the eyelashes to avoid further irritating the eye further. Start in the inside corner, and allow your pet the chance to close his eye before gently wiping downwards towards the outside corner.

To remove heavy matter or copious discharge in and around the eye, use a warm, wet cotton pad or ultra-soft cotton paper towel. Hold it gently against the eye, allowing it time to soften any hardened matter. Gently wipe the inside of the lid to remove discharge on the eyeball, being careful not to introduce any dirt or crust into the eye. Then remove the remaining matter on the outside lashes. Repeat as often as needed. Do not allow the eye to remain crusted-over and shut. This will encourage infection, possibly damaging the eye or tear duct permanently.

Follow cleaning with an application of natural eye drops made from a dilution of six drops of *Calendula Extract* into a couple of ounces of distilled water. For very irritated or dry eyes, add 200 IUs of natural *Vitamin E Oil* to the eye drops, shaking the solution well before each use. Or apply a few drops directly to the inside of the lower eyelid every other day. Be careful not to scratch the eye. Blinking will disperse the Vitamin E. A few drops of *Golden Seal Extract* can also be added to eye drops, if infection is present. This will also help to open up tear ducts and to encourage natural lubrication.

Always supplement with herbs to strengthen and cleanse the eye to increase resistance to allergens and infections, and to support successful anti-inflammatory and antihistamine action. Proper nutritional and herbal supplementation can prevent and even reverse cataracts—a common side-effect of chronic eye irritation.

Cataracts also occur in some cats. Diabetes seems to be the most prevalent cause of feline cataracts. Irritants and toxins, from environmental and dietary sources, can also damage sensitive eye lens tissues, causing them to "scar" or cloud over. A lack of nutrients such as Vitamin A, E, and Zinc (often depleted during chronic illness) can also encourage the formation of cataracts. Along with proper nutrition, I have successfully reversed cataracts with homeopathic Silica 200C daily for four weeks, then Silica 1M weekly for four weeks, then Silica 10M weekly for four more weeks. The higher doses of Silica should be used under the supervision of an experienced practitioner.

Corneal Ulcers are frequently seen in cats who have suffered from inhaled, ingested, or environmental allergies, especially dust. Skirmishes with other cats and genetic problems, such as turned-in lashes, can also injure the eye. Lack of tears, scratching, and rubbing of the eyes, as well as nutritional deficiencies, contribute to the development of ulcers on the outer protective layer of the eyeball. Once your veterinarian has diagnosed this problem, corneal ulcers can often be quickly reversed with twice daily applications of natural Vitamin E (d-Alpha, not dl-Alpha) directly to the inner eyelid, so blinking can spread it over the entire eye. When there is no tear production or a blockage of the tear ducts apply a high-quality, natural tear solution to prevent drying.

Upper Respiratory Problems can be the most frequently seen chronic symptom and can be very difficult to reverse. Environmental pollutants, including second-hand smoke, easily irritate lung and nasal tissues. Cats are prone to inhaling foreign objects due to their curiosity about everything in their environments. If there is excessive sneezing or nasal discharge that does not respond to natural remedies, consult your veterinarian to determine if a foreign object is the cause.

Pneumonia and pleural effusion (trapped fluid pockets in the lungs) frequently is associated with chronic immunosuppressive diseases, including bacterial infections, FIP, feline leukemia, and ruptured lymphatic vessels. Follow recommendations for edema control. Homeopathic remedies such as *Apis*, *Lycopodium*, and *Arsenicum* are effective.

Asthma can also occur in cats, as an allergic reaction, or as the result of a severe respiratory infection. The homeopathic remedies *Aconite*, *Bryonia*, or *Thuja* can be effective.
    Daily cleaning of the nostrils with a warm, damp cloth to keep discharge and crusted mucus clear of the nasal passages will help facilitate healing. Homeopathic *Spongia* is a

wonderful expectorant and lung toner. *Lobelia* is a standard herb for improved lung function. Other homeopathic and herbal supplementation can successfully address more specific symptoms.

TEETH AND GUMS: PROPER DENTAL CARE

Gum problems (gingivitis), abscesses, and bad teeth are the most common mouth diseases. Proper oral care is vital to good health. Poor teeth and painful gums make chewing difficult and painful, inhibiting proper digestion. Food is swallowed whole and is more difficult to break down further for assimilation. Vital nutrients are lost, regardless of how good the diet is.

If chewing is too painful and your cat refuses to eat, the lack of food can quickly exacerbate an immune weakness. I have seen too many cats starving to death because of bad teeth. Bacteria, which flourish in the warm, moist environment provided by the mouth, feed on the yeast and sugar in a cat's diet, and can trigger a severe systemic infection if not addressed.

Weekly cleaning of your cat's mouth, availability of a high-quality dry kibble (home prepared if preferred), and bones will help keep the teeth free of tartar. Proper maintenance of your cat's teeth and mouth is the best, safest route to take to ensure that your cat's teeth won't be the cause of disease or death.

Examining and Brushing Your Cat's Teeth

To prevent tooth decay and oral problems, examine your cat's teeth weekly. Check for any signs of redness, ulceration, or discharge between the teeth and around the mouth and tongue. Note any cracked or chipped teeth and check to be sure that the teeth are secure in the gums. See your veterinarian immediately when you observe abscessed, cracked, loose, or dangling teeth.

Follow this weekly examination by a brushing with a child's toothbrush. You can also wrap a thin wet washcloth around your index finger and rub the teeth clean, which some cats might prefer to a toothbrush, especially in the beginning. It can take time for your pet to get used to a toothbrush. Apply a very small amount of natural adult or children's fluoride-free toothpaste. If you suspect a gum infection, use toothpaste that includes *Tea Tree*, *Grapefruit*, or *Golden Seal Extract*. Start with the toothbrush at the back of the mouth, working your way to the front teeth. Try to open the mouth slightly so you can get behind the teeth and to the back bottom molars, a prime decay area. Wipe away any leftover toothpaste with a wet cloth. You do not need to use a lot of toothpaste, so there should not be much left over to wipe.

Rinse the brush in clean water and, using the clean brush *with water in the bristles*, remove any remaining toothpaste from between the teeth. It is safe for your cat to swallow a little of the natural toothpaste. Many actually enjoy the taste, but do not overdo it. You don't need to foam up your cat's mouth to get it clean. Pets don't like the foam and will fight you.

For any accumulated tartar that brushing has not removed, use a dental scraper available in many pet catalogues. You can remove heavy tartar by applying a flat-edged scraper to the crown of the tartar build-up (at the gum line) and flicking it downward. It will usually come off in a large chunk. Try not to allow your pet to swallow these chunks if possible. Once the majority of tartar has been cleaned, weekly brushing and proper diet should keep your cat's teeth tartar-free and pearly white. Allowing your cat to chew on a hard-baked turkey neck, which has first steamed soft so the bones break down easily, cleans the surface of the teeth and stimulates the gums.

Always approach your cat gently when introducing anything new, especially dental cleanings. Start by getting them used to you rubbing a clean finger over their teeth and gums. Once they have become comfortable with this you can proceed to brushing. Never force your cat to do anything, but rather slowly introduce them to it. If you force them, they will only fight you and then avoid you in the future. Use a "rescue" or calming flower essence remedy if needed.

Yearly teeth cleaning under anesthesia may weaken your cat's immune system and interfere with their good health. Many cats had a reoccurrence of various chronic symptoms shortly after having their teeth cleaned under anesthesia. There is always a risk of dying during surgical procedures. Your cat should be put under anesthesia for life-threatening conditions only, not for elective procedures.

Most problems can be prevented, but, if needed, oral problems generally respond well to home care:

- *Bad breath* is mainly associated with poor dental hygiene. Most cases of bad breath originate in the digestive tract, not from tartar build-up. If dental hygiene does not get rid of the offensive odor, use one of the detoxification methods and make sure your cat is fed a nutritious diet.

- *Painful gums* respond to a dose of homeopathic *Hypericum* a few minutes before cleaning. Also apply *Clove Teething Gel* after remedy. Continue with the *Hypericum* twice per day, until gums are normal. *Mercurius* is beneficial for cats that are very irritable with swollen gums that bleed easily.

- *Foreign bodies* can become lodged in a cat's mouth. You can usually remove the object yourself if your cat is willing, although a veterinarian should remove string, rubber bands, or ribbon caught in the throat or already in the stomach.

- *Gingivitis* can consist of gum inflammation, receding or infected gums. An effective natural antiseptic and antibiotic mouth rinse can be made by adding six drops each of *Golden*

Seal Root Extract and *Calendula Extract* to two ounces of distilled water. Brush away food with a wet toothbrush or cloth and rinse the mouth out daily after meals.

- *Plasma Cell Gingivitis* occurs when red, friable gums grow over and cover the teeth. This type of gingivitis will eventually prevent the cat from eating. Anti-inflammatory herbs such as *Yucca Extract* can reduce swelling and discomfort, while homeopathic *Thuja* can cause the infected tissue to recede.

- *Prevention of tooth decay* can be accomplished through weekly cleaning and basic nutritional support. Raw soft bones, such as chicken, pork, and lamb bones can cause the cat to choke and are detrimental to the digestive tract, but small hard-baked turkey necks or beef shank pieces or knuckles provide a good surface to chew on. Chewing helps remove tartar from the surface of the teeth, as well as stimulates the gums. The homeopathic remedy, *Calcarea Phos.*, both in a lower daily dose (10X to 3C) and/or higher potencies (200C), given weekly can help prevent tartar, but brushing is still the best method.

- *Ulcers of the mouth*, especially the lips, can either be secondary responses to infection or an autoimmune response. Cats with FIP, feline leukemia, or feline rhinotracheitis are especially prone to the development of oral ulcers. Anti-inflammatory herbs such as *Yucca Extract* can reduce swelling and discomfort, while homeopathic *Mercurius* and *Arsenicum* can help heal the ulcerated tissue. Use *Hepar Sulph.* if the ulcer is very moist and aggravated, or predominantly in the corners of the mouth.

SKIN AND COAT CARE

Proper nutrition, exercise, and grooming will guarantee your cat healthy skin and a luxurious coat. Many imbalances and chronic conditions will first appear as skin and coat symptoms. Supporting a healthy skin and coat condition starts from the inside out. Proper diet and supplementation will do more to prevent these conditions than brushing and bathing. Grooming and less shedding reduces hairballs.

Proper grooming cannot be underestimated for stimulating waste and parasite removal. Grooming also promotes circulation and tissue repair by bringing more nutrients to the skin and coat. A daily brushing, followed by a rubdown with a damp terry cloth towel can work wonders to maintain good skin and coat condition and reduce shedding. Find a good grooming book to learn more about the proper techniques and tools needed for your particular breed or mix. Avoid shampooing too frequently, as this can strip the coat of oils or can stimulate over-production of oils, resulting in a greasy coat.

Acne, Pimples, Eczema, Cysts, Fatty Tumors, and Warts can be reversed with a combination of herbs including *Red Clover, Stinging Nettle Leaf, Cleavers Herb, Yellow Dock Root, Burdock Root*, and *Yarrow Flowers*. Together, these herbs help clean the blood and lymphatic system. They also improve a pet's metabolism by carrying more blood and nutrients to the cells and help eliminate cellular waste. This improved metabolism decreases irritation and scratching, while stimulating tissue repair. This combination of herbs is indicated for both greasy and dry skin conditions.

The homeopathic remedy *Apis* addresses rashes and general irritation that prompts scratching or rubbing. *Thuja* and/or *Arsenicum* help reverse warts, cysts, and fatty growths. *Calcarea Carb.* is an outstanding homeopathic remedy to eliminate warts. *Silica* will eliminate growths under the skin, including cysts, abscesses, or ulcers. *Hepar Sulph* is indicated for weepy, painful areas.

Greasy Coat and Offensive Odors can be addressed through proper grooming. To make a solution to eliminate offensive odors, cut up one lemon. Boil it in one quart of distilled water for five minutes. Reduce the heat and simmer, covered, for twenty minutes. Leave the lemon in the water overnight. Strain and refrigerate. Rinse your cat with the solution daily or spray on irritated areas. Let the cat's coat air dry. The lemon solution has antiseptic properties but, for additional infection control, add twenty drops of *Golden Seal* or *Grapefruit Extract*. The homeopathic remedy *Psorinum* is beneficial when the skin has an acrid odor with acne, discharging pustules, or hot spots that are slow to heal. *Psorinum* reduces the production of oils from the sebaceous glands, which are associated with a greasy coat and sebaceous cysts. In this condition, itching is aggravated by warmth, yet the cat is sensitive to cold and seeks warmth.

Dry Coat, Dandruff, Cracked Skin, and Thin Skin should be addressed with herbal formulas containing Milk Thistle Seed (for liver toxicity), Yellow Dock Root (for fatty acid metabolism), Burdock Root (for blood purification), Echinacea Root (antibacterial), Sarsaparilla Root (for disorders associated with hormonal balance) and Oregon Grape Root (for liver metabolism). Arsenicum is a good general homeopathic choice, while Sepia works well on irritations, especially cracked toes and feet that itch badly with no relief from scratching. Psorinum is beneficial when the cat's coat seems dirty and dingy, and is brittle and lackluster no matter how much grooming is performed. Topical application of Jojoba Oil conditioner can reduce dryness temporarily, while herbs and nutrients are used to build up in the body and reverse the underlying imbalance.

Hair Loss, Poor Coat Condition, and Excessive Scratching respond well to *Turmeric Root, Black Catechu, Grindelia Flowers, Licorice Root, Ginkgo Leaf, African Devil's Claw, Yarrow,* and *Lobelia*. This herbal combination protects the liver and aids in the detoxification of allergens, which may be at the root of the problem. This combination is beneficial when food allergies are suspected, especially symptoms involving protein metabolism. Watch for excessive licking of the feet and belly (urea toxicity). The homeopathic remedy *Arsenicum* is good for general hair loss. *Sulphur* addresses ringworm or other circular-patch irritations, which are often the cause of scratching and hair loss.

Licking is a serious concern for many cat owners. Excessive licking is not only irritating to the owner, but it will quickly exhaust your pet. Vital healing energy is redirected to address the fatigue, rather than to supporting tissue repair and immune stimulation. Cats with short or long hair, or who are shedding excessively, are also prone to hairballs and digestive upsets.

Although normal daily self-grooming includes licking the body clean, obsessive or chronic licking can lead to skin eruptions. Homeopathic *Arsenicum* works best for constant licking, especially when a build-up of urea is suspected. *Calcarea Phos.* can be beneficial, when given frequently, to help reduce licking. *Apis* is for rashly skin. Herbs, such as *St. John's Wort* and *Chamomile*, help reduce the anxiety often associated with excessive licking. Try Flower Essences, such as *Rescue* or *Mimulus*, which are good for obsessive licking.

DIGESTIVE AND GLANDULAR SYSTEMS

Many cat owners complain that it is difficult to find a diet for their cat that doesn't cause side-effects. Digestive disorders, such as a lack of appetite, vomiting, stool changes, or hairballs, are the second-most common complaint I hear from cat owners. The first most common complaint is urinary problems. Digestive disorders may be prompted by allergies, environmental toxins, chemical agents, vaccines, and pest control products. Digestive enzymes are commonly used to suppress some digestive imbalances. Although they can be beneficial, for long-term symptom reversal, you will have to address the actual imbalance.

Chronic digestive disorder symptoms can develop into more serious dis-ease, such as bowel, pancreatic, or liver cancer, diabetes, and bowel obstruction. Also, the inability to assimilate nutrients can lead to muscle loss and starvation. Holistic animal care can reverse these issues quickly and effectively. It will also help to prevent such disorders from ever occurring, by controlling and reversing accidental toxicity before the reaction becomes too severe.

Proper Feeding Guidelines

How you feed your cat is as important as what you feed her. Cats fed only one meal per day often develop weight or digestive problems. The single daily meal puts too much stress on the digestive tract. It's far better to feed your cat half that amount, two times a day, allowing the body to digest and assimilate the food more thoroughly.

Kittens from weaning to three months of age should be fed four meals per day, or you can allow them to feed freely throughout the day.

Sick cats or kittens from three to six months of age should be fed three meals per day, or you can allow them to feed freely throughout the day.

Adult cats should be fed twice per day or free-fed.

I do recommend freestyle feeding, giving your cat unlimited access to food. Many cats prefer to eat at their leisure, but they can overeat and, if your cat's feeding behavior changes, you will be less likely to notice. It is better to put out one day's food at a time. Check every week to make sure that your cat is assimilating her food well and is sustaining her normal weight. You should be able to feel ribs—but not see them.

Use ceramic, glass, or stainless steel feeding dishes and water bowls: Your cat is less likely to develop bacteria or viral infections. Such bowls don't scratch the way plastic ones do. Aluminum dishes can give a cat aluminum poisoning—cats may ingest slivers of aluminum while they are eating, or you may scrape off pieces of aluminum while you are mixing the meal with a fork.

Provide plenty of fresh, filtered water. Never use tap water, which may contain contaminants. Be sure that the bowl is heavy and can't be tipped over. Also keep the water cool and clean of debris.

Appetite Problems, especially loss of appetite, can occur during curative responses. Cats are more particular about what they will eat than are dogs, and tend to self-fast when needed. If your cat is not eating, check to see if he has a fever, or if his fluid intake has changed. Either symptom could indicate that something serious is going on. Also, assess the level of stress, which can also interfere with appetite. Sometimes, a loss of appetite can have several causes.

For nutritional support, feed up to 100 mg. of *B-Complex vitamins* per day, regardless of your cat's weight. This, in addition to a short fast (if you haven't done one recently) can quickly stimulate the appetite. Often, a lack of appetite is the result of a toxic overload.

Try a few doses of *Arsenicum* (in general), *Nux Vomica* (when loss of appetite is accompanied by one or more of the following symptoms: nausea, vomiting, stool problems, or flatulence). *Belladonna* can be used for nausea, empty retching, and vomiting as well as for your cat's refusal to drink water. A dose or two daily, *especially fifteen minutes prior to feeding,* can also help stimulate appetite. Several flower essences, especially *Mimulus*, *Star of Bethlehem*, and *Rock Rose* or a combination act to minimize stress in general and can often settle a cat sufficiently so that he will want to eat.

Bacterial Enteritis is responsible for many cases of fever, depression, and diarrhea in cats. Two types of bacteria are responsible: *Campylobacter fetus jejuni* and *Salmonella*. These bacterial infections are usually secondary to other gastrointestinal diseases, such as FIP, or an immune depressive condition such as feline leukemia. *Campylobacter* can be spread to humans, especially babies. *Salmonella* can become fatal if allowed to continue, since it can spread to liver and lungs. Monitor fluid intake carefully and use appropriate herbal or homeopathic remedies to address digestive upsets.

Bad Breath is usually thought to be the result of poor dental hygiene and accumulated tartar. Certainly, you should rule out any broken, abscessed teeth or gingivitis (inflamed gum disease), and always properly care for your cat's teeth and gums. If this does not resolve the odor, address toxicity in your cat's digestive tract, which can result in bad odor escaping through the mouth.

Old fecal material, poor-quality food, or by-products in the food that are not easily digested can result in what I refer to as "digestive composting." The lack of digestive enzymes and lack of water can also aid the composting process in the intestines. Food backs up in the digestive tract, fermenting and breaking down slowly just like in a compost heap. The results are the same. When you turn over compost, you release trapped gases caused by the natural process of organic decomposition. These gases can be quite offensive, as you possibly have experienced if your cat has ever been flatulent (same process—rear exit). These gases are released from the digestive system through the mouth. If you try to get rid of the odor by cleaning your cat's teeth or giving her breath mints, the odor will quickly return. Homeopathic *Arsenicum* and *Nux Vomica* are excellent remedies for odor elimination. Dietary *Garlic* and *Parsley* work well to rebalance the digestive tract. *Garlic* encourages proper elimination and is antiseptic. *Parsley* or *liquid chlorophyll* will reduce garlicky odor as well as digestive swamp gas. If the cat's tongue is coated, detoxify with herbs and homeopathic remedies for yeast over-growth.

Colitis and Irritable Bowel Syndrome are common symptoms associated with chronic hairballs, parasites (*giardia* or *coccidia*) or allergies, especially yeast and other food allergies. The constant stress of other chronic conditions can also result in diarrhea, constipation (or both), mucous-covered stools, flatulence, and even slight blood in the stool. *Nux Vomica* and *Arsenicum* are a great homeopathic combination to use initially. *Silica* and *Nux Vomica* (used alternately) can promote the expulsion of hairballs. *Phosphorus* helps to eliminate blood in the stool.

Digestive enzymes can also be appropriate, but I recommend that you limit their use to a few weeks at a time. Excessive use of enzymes can imbalance digestion further. Calming herbs, especially *Wild Oats* and *St. John's Wort*, are also helpful.

Do supplement with a variety of bulk-producing ingredients including whole grains, fruits, and vegetables to stimulate evacuation and improve bowel function. Avoid psyllium, which may be too harsh when used alone. *Yucca* is a wonderfully soothing herb, as are *Aloe* and *Slippery Elm Bark*. If this regimen does not settle things, seek more specific support under each particular topic.

Constipation and Diarrhea are common symptoms associated with stress or toxicity. Some pets alternate between constipation and diarrhea, whereas others will have either one or the other. Constipation can weaken the body, due to improper elimination of waste products. Rather than being eliminated, these toxins continue to be reabsorbed through the colon into the blood. Diarrhea is often associated with food allergies. But I have also seen it caused by allergies or parasitic infections, which irritate the cat's skin, so that she constantly scratches or bites it—all that nervous energy just churns up the bowel.

Feline Megacolon, a condition in which nerves in the muscular walls of the colon do not function properly, can result from chronic bowel obstructions, injury, or chronic disease. Some cats, such as the Manx, can inherit a neurological weakness in which peristalsis of the colon is impaired.

Several factors can contribute to bowel upsets, including medications often used during crisis, such as antibiotics, steroids, and antihistamines. First eliminate any possible culprits, including:

- An ingested piece of sting, ribbon, or rubber band
- Hard-to-digest cat food ingredients, such as "plant cellulose," which is often soy castings, peanut shells, or recycled paper pulp, and food preservatives like ethoxyquin
- Lack of exercise, especially with six hours or more of prolonged confinement
- Inadequate amounts of fluids imbibed
- Excessive ingestion of fur due to licking and chewing

• Poor sources of dietary fiber (i.e., the paper pulp mentioned above)

Psyllium Seed or Husk is the most commonly used fiber to help regulate bowel movement, but often when used by itself, it can be too harsh on the digestive tract. I highly recommend combining it with fruits and vegetables and other fiber sources such as *carrots, apple fiber and pectin, guar gum* (a misunderstood, but excellent source of natural fiber that swells to retain water), and *bran*. Chinese mushrooms, such as *Shiitake* and *Reishi*, have long been noted for their fiber content, as well as their curative potential in reversing chronic colon conditions such as pre-cancerous growths, which, when irritated, can trigger diarrhea. Cooked *oatmeal*, added to meals or given alone with vegetable, fish, or meat broth, provides an excellent source of fiber. It also has detoxifying properties to help eliminate old fecal material from the bowels. (See Fasting.)

Old fecal material can become toxic (especially with bacterial infection) and can push the body to eliminate the irritation, so that diarrhea results. Supplement with potent doses of a high-quality *Garlic* supplement (500 mg. to 1000 mg. per day) for natural antibiotic support. Homeopathic *Arsenicum* (for general symptoms), *China* (for debilitating fluid loss or parasites), and *Nux Vomica* (for vomiting and/or appetite loss) are effective in relieving diarrhea and associated symptoms.

Use herbal remedies like *Yucca* and/or *Calendula Extract*, *Liquid Chlorophyll*, and *Slippery Elm Extract or Powder* to soothe irritated intestinal tissues. Be sure that your cat's fluid intake is maintained, as diarrhea can quickly dehydrate him. Adding a half teaspoon of *raw honey* to fluids or herbal preparations will not only be soothing to an irritated colon, but is also an antiseptic and will provide energy for a weakened cat.

Dehydration can be caused by excessive vomiting or diarrhea and will quickly shut down bodily functions, especially the body's attempt to detoxify itself when an imbalance of nutrients and electrolytes occur. Cats are prone to developing secondary symptoms, such as urinary tract blockages or intestinal disorders, if they become dehydrated.

To check for dehydration, grab the skin from the back of the neck between your forefinger and thumb, pulling it gently upwards and releasing it. Pulled skin should return to normal within a second or two. If it takes longer, the animal is dehydrated. If the skin remains in a peak and doesn't snap back, consult with your veterinarian immediately for subcutaneous fluid replacement therapy. In all other instances you can easily re-hydrate your cat orally with a feeding syringe or by encouraging fluid intake. Provide one ounce of water per one pound of body weight per day. Electrolyte solutions can be added to the water if the cat seems weakened by the dehydration or is constitutionally weak to begin with. Keep a dehydrated cat quiet, in a cool dark area.

Esophageal Disorders are very common in cats, particularly in certain breeds. Symptoms include difficulty in swallowing and the regurgitation of solid food soon after eating.

Megaesophagus is the general term for an enlarged esophagus, a condition in which it is impossible for food to move through the esophagus and into the stomach. The regurgitated food is undigested and often sausage or tube-shaped. If your cat shows signs of this condition, feed her canned, semi-solid, or liquid food. Several smaller meals per day work best.

Esophagitis is a condition in which the esophagus is inflamed, due to injury, ingestion of caustic substances, acid reflux, or allergies. Appetite and weight losses are common symptoms. *Esophagitis* responds well to the anti-inflammatory herbal extract, *Yucca*.

Esophageal Obstruction can occur as secondary to tumors, strictures, or ingestion of foreign objects, especially bones. Consult your veterinarian immediately if you suspect an that there is an obstruction.

Motion Sickness can be a behavioral issue. Many emotions, including fear, abandonment, aggression, or nervousness can trigger motion sickness. This is an acute reaction to motion in a car, boat, or plane. This includes *perceived motion*, the result of seizures or inner ear imbalance caused by infections. (See Seizures; Ears.) Utilize an herbal combination of *Skullcap, St. John's Wort, Chamomile Flowers, California Poppy, Wild Oats*, and *Valerian Root* an hour or so before the trip. These herbs will help to normalize and to restore the nervous system while providing a sense of calm, without the sludgy side-effects of drugs. Homeopathic *Petroleum* and *Nux Vomica* are excellent anti-nausea remedies to be taken for travel sickness. Symptoms such as hysterical panting, excessive salivation, and restlessness, which commonly occur just prior to vomiting, respond well to a few doses the day before traveling, thirty minutes *and again at* fifteen minutes prior to departure, and again as needed during the trip. Flower combinations for "fear" or "rescue" can also help reduce stress-related symptoms.

Organs and Glands of the Digestive and Immune Systems

Liver imbalance is often at the root of digestive and glandular disorders, especially those involving the immune system. It is vital that you are careful about what you feed your cat, as the liver can become congested and burdened. If you suspect liver dis-ease, immediately eliminate all yeast from your pet's diet and treats, and stop all flea relief supplements (garlic works better).

The liver is a primary organ of the digestive, eliminatory, and immune systems, which marshal the body's defenses against toxins, and are involved in tissue repair. The care and support of your cat's liver must be a basic concern if you are to be successful in supporting optimum health and wellness for your cat. The liver is responsible for a great deal of bodily functions—from metabolism of life-sustaining nutrients passing through the intestines, to detoxification of toxic chemicals, poisons, and drugs circulating in the blood. It is vital that the liver not be allowed to deteriorate or become stressed. Fluids can build up within the abdominal cavity due to bleeding, resulting in anemia and pain. Portal congestion increases resistance to blood flow through the liver, starving it of nutrients and fluids. Luckily, the liver is remarkable because it can rejuvenate itself, as long as there is some healthy tissue remaining.

I have seen cats come back from the brink of death after an accidental poisoning, as long as the liver was protected and supported during their recovery. Unfortunately, traditional medical care often overlooks the importance of specific liver support during illness, especially during a viral infection. Many kittens who have had FIP (Feline Infectious Peritonitis) and recovered *without* holistic support, later developed liver disease. However, kittens that were supported holistically never suffer liver distress and secondary symptoms such as abdominal distention, loss of appetite, or weight loss.

Cats lack *glucuronyl transferase*, an enzyme responsible for the detoxification of certain drugs. Because they lack this enzyme, cats are dangerously sensitive to aspirin and its herbal twin, white willow bark, and acetaminophen. Never give any over-the-counter drugs to your cat without veterinarian consent. Carefully read the labels of all medications, including "natural" pain and anti-inflammatory drugs. Although it is common knowledge that cats lack this enzyme, several pet product manufacturers use white willow bark in their feline formulas. Many herbal preparations have proven helpful in rebuilding the liver. See the recommendations for maintaining a healthy immune system.

The Pancreas is a gland that can cause digestive upsets when it malfunctions. It is primarily responsible for proper enzyme digestion of carbohydrates, fats, and protein. The pancreatic enzymes produced here mix with other enzymes to facilitate digestion. The pancreas plays a vital role in the production of the hormones insulin and glucagon. Improper pancreatic function can lead to several diseases, including diabetes and cancer.

Diet is the biggest culprit in pancreatic dysfunction. Chemical or viral exposure, parasitic infestation, and even trauma from a blow can also have severe consequences. Certain commonly prescribed drugs, antibiotics, and corticosteroids can damage the pancreas or cause a malfunction.

Nausea and vomiting (especially of partially digested food), or fatty, off-colored stools are primary symptoms of pancreatic malfunction. Loss of appetite, with excessive salivation and marked pain in the right lower rib quadrant, can indicate pancreatic dysfunction. Cats who have been fed poor-quality diets containing rancid animal fats or meats, or those who have been allowed to become overweight, can easily have a pancreatic flare-up. Diet is the best way to prevent pancreatic problems. Continued use of toxic foods, chemical substances, medications, and exposure to stress will lead to reoccurrence of pancreatic symptoms. General holistic care should be followed, and secondary symptoms should be specifically addressed.

Diabetes is mentioned here because it is another disease that can be frequently traced back to a history of digestive problems associated with pancreatic dysfunction. I believe that the relation between blood sugar stabilization (or lack of it) and sensitivities resulting in digestive upsets has yet to be fully appreciated by veterinarians. I first perceived that many cats *finally* responded to medical treatment *for their digestive symptoms* only after they were diagnosed with diabetes (often later in their lives), when their blood sugar was stabilized through insulin and diet.

Adhering to a holistic animal care lifestyle when symptoms present themselves early in your pet's life will help prevent a diabetic condition from developing. Herbal support can also be very successful in reducing the amount of insulin needed. I have seen a combination of herbs, in addition to proper diet and supplementation, wean many cats completely off insulin. A formula of *Devil's Club Root and Bark, Indian Jambul Seed, Dandelion Leaf and Root, Uva Ursi Leaf,* and *Turmeric Root* strengthens the pancreas, promoting better production and utilization of insulin. This herbal formula also normalizes and restores the organs and glands associated with carbohydrate and sugar metabolism, which are needed for curative energy. Re-synthesis of glycogen promotes greater balance of glucose, and is indicated in both hyper- and hypoglycemia.

Spleen function is frequently overlooked or misunderstood. This valuable organ removes and destroys worn out, defective, or misshapen red blood cells, and thus reduces toxic build-up in the body. The spleen also harvests some antibodies needed in the fight against infection. *Astragalus Root* and *Calendula* are wonderful herbs for the spleen.

Adrenal Gland malfunction can be very common in cats who also exhibit allergic reactions, especially chronic skin conditions. Frequently, this malfunction can be caused by previous cycles of corticosteroids, the very drugs that are most commonly used to suppress inflammatory-related symptoms, including digestive upsets.

Cushing's Disease, a condition associated with adrenal malfunction, is not common in cats, but bears many similarities to symptoms linked to FIP or feline leukemia. Overproduction of naturally occurring corticosteroids cause chronic symptoms such as increased food or water consumption, frequent elimination, stress or exercise intolerance, "allergies," and reduction in muscle tone, especially in the belly. A potbelly is a common characteristic of this disease.

Addison's Disease or hypoadrenocorticism is caused by inadequate amounts of circulating corticosteroids, the opposite condition to Cushing's Disease. It is very rare in cats, although it can be frequently triggered by immunosuppressive drug therapy. Inadequate amounts of circulating corticosteroids creates an imbalance of fluid and electrolytes, and can be life-threatening, because decreasing levels of potassium and sodium will cause stress on the heart. Clinical symptoms look like gastrointestinal stress—vomiting, diarrhea, and dehydration. Problems with appetite and weight loss can be common, although overconsumption of water might be present as well.

Herbal formulas containing *Siberian Ginseng Root, Chinese Schizandra Berry, Damiana Leaf, Kola Nut, Wild Oats, Licorice Root, Skullcap Herb,* and *Prickly Ash Bark* work well together to restore integrity to the adrenal glands, thus promoting greater energy and stamina, while building up the body's adaptogenic abilities against stress. *Astragalus Root* is a general herbal restorative for the adrenal gland. These herbs are nutritive and act as a tonic to the adrenals, the nerve cells, and tissue.

Homeopathic *Adrenaline* (epinephrine) is also helpful. Use this only in lower potencies such as 3X to 6X and for no more than two weeks at a time, with a month off in-between uses. It is best used with other remedies and supportive supplements. Some cats may become very excitable when this remedy is administered. Use *Adrenaline* with caution. *Arsenicum* (for general adrenal malfunction, and secondary symptoms), *Iodum* (helps avoid stress on heart or skin), and *Silica* (helps counter improper assimilation of nutrients, reduces keloid growths on skin, and soothes anxiety) are all appropriate homeopathic remedies to use for adrenal support.

Thyroid Problems can be very common to animals with chronic skin or weight conditions. Siamese and Persian cats are very prone to thyroid imbalances. The thyroid influences metabolism, encouraging proper nutrient and oxygen utilization. Often, glandular imbalance can actually be caused by previous cycles of corticosteroids and other immune-suppressive medications.

Hypothyroidism, a condition much rarer in cats than in dogs, generally is associated with immune dysfunction. It results in iodine deficiencies, and the underdevelopment or malfunction of the thyroid and pituitary glands. Symptoms include lethargy, intolerance of cold, dull coat, color change or hair loss, and poor appetite—often accompanied by weight gain, allergies, eye problems, seizures, and arthritis.

Hyperthyroidism—Cats are more prone to Hyperthyroidism, which can lead to anxiety, obsessive behavior, withdrawal, and wasting disease—rapid weight loss due to muscle deterioration, regardless of great hunger. Cats, especially those between eight and ten years of age, are prone to tumor development on the thyroid gland, which can lead to breathing difficulties. *Yucca*, in the standardized extract form, seems to help the glands respond more quickly to nutritional support. *Sarsaparilla Root* is an excellent herbal remedy for the thyroid gland that helps to balance hormone regulation.

Use homeopathic remedies such as *Thyroidinum* (to rebalance thyroid function and address general symptoms); *Belladonna* (for thyroid toxemia, i.e., a pet who is easily excited, with general thyroid symptoms); *Calcarea Carb.* (for pets who are easily chilled, thyroid dysfunction with pituitary involvement, facial eruptions, or a flabby, distended belly with an aversion to animal protein and fat); *Spongia* (for gland enlargement, goiter); *Hydrastis* (for goiter, nervousness, and autoimmune problems related to thyroid dysfunction); *Iodum* (for loss of weight and flesh regardless of strong hunger).

Veterinary testing for thyroid or adrenal hormonal (cortisol) levels will benefit you in making decisions about your cat's care. Thyroid and adrenal gland function is fundamental to many wellness issues. Utilize medication only when appropriate for you and your pet, especially if nothing else seems to work. Long-term natural support can reduce or even eliminate the need for chemicals, and is safe to use in conjunction with medications.

Once you start on medication, it can be more difficult to eliminate the need to continue the drugs. Unless the situation is life-threatening, try holistic animal care first. Pets who have not responded to natural modalities are often diagnosed with deeper glandular malfunctions. Short-term medication may be all that is needed to stimulate the overall curative process.

There are many wonderful glandular products on the market today. I prefer *Glandular Extracts* (in powder or tablet form) to homeopathic ones, but please do not disregard a homeopathic combination with a potentized glandular *in addition to* a tableted form. Homeopathic glandulars work on a deeper level that is certainly beneficial to overall support, whereas tableted glandulars actually "feed" the gland directly and provide more substantial support in reversing glandular weakness. *Multi-glandulars* (a combination of several) are beneficial in supporting the weaker gland, but make sure that it is of sufficient potency in the particular gland that you need to stimulate and support. Add another single glandular product to the multiple, if needed.

General Symptom Reversal for Digestive Disorders

I have found homeopathy to be highly effective in reversing acute stomachaches, liver inflammation, and appetite or stool changes. It is also effective in relieving the underlying stress that often accompanies digestive disorders.

These are the homeopathic remedies that I prefer for digestive disorders:

Arsenicum is used for digestive imbalances or general toxicity of the digestive system, and will take care of most symptoms, especially those with liver or spleen involvement, or after a season of chemical pesticide use (i.e., flea/tick control products, especially those with a monthly dose application). *Arsenicum* can help reverse energy loss due to feline leukemia.

Nux Vomica also addresses the majority of digestive imbalances, including gas, vomiting, stool problems (especially alternating between constipation and diarrhea), or lack of appetite. It is a good complement to *Arsenicum*, especially when poor-quality food or chronic drug use is suspected. *Nux Vomica* works well for kittens with FIP.

Carbo Veg is helpful when the cat is overweight, has chronic stool problems, seems to have trouble digesting well, and burps soon after eating. It is extremely beneficial when used with *Nux Vomica*, in alternating doses.

Belladonna is for the sudden onset of gastrointestinal symptoms. It can be used initially, then tapered off slowly and replaced with a more specific remedy. It is also indicated for acute colic and pancreatic imbalances resulting in a "fatty" stool.

Iodum is for primary liver and spleen enlargement and pancreatic disease. The stool is whitish and fatty—frequently with a frothy diarrhea or blood. It is excellent for the anxiety and worry that is exhibited by a cat who is not fed soon enough. It also reduces thyroid goiter.

Herbal remedies can support prevention or reversal of many symptoms associated with digestive disorders. They can increase digestion or assimilation, and stabilize appetite. The herbs themselves are very nutritive as well.

Many cats cannot tolerate herbs on an empty stomach—in fact, herbs may have been creating some of the pet's digestive distress. When cats have digestive upsets, it is best to give these remedies with a little food until the remedies are better tolerated. It is also advisable to seek better-quality herbs. Poor-quality herbs or chemically based solvents used to process cheaper herbal products may also trigger a reaction, no matter whether you give the remedy with food or not.

Yucca extract provides natural steroidal saponins, effectively reducing inflammation within the digestive system: the esophagus, the stomach, the intestinal lining, the thyroid or adrenal glands, as well as the liver, gall bladder, spleen, and pancreas. A reduction in excessive peristalsis (the squeezing response of the intestines to process and move digested material toward the colon) can help relieve diarrhea due to allergic and inflammatory responses. The intestinal pockets, ulcerations, and inflamed intestinal valves (that block passage of matter) that are often associated with esophageal disorders, colitis, or bacteria enteritis, have also responded well to *Yucca* supplementation.

Garlic is a miraculous herb for digestive complaints. Not only is it an antiseptic and a natural antibiotic, it effectively supports proper digestion and colon health through its anti-parasitic and anti-yeast properties. It can be used to reverse flatulence, bad breath, general diarrhea, and fatty stool deposits, and supports the processing of ingested hair.

Peppermint Leaf or *Fenugreek Seed* helps reduce intestinal gas and cramping, prevents fatty deposits and colic, repairs digestive tissue ulcerations, and fights infection.

Dandelion Leaf is an excellent liver and gall bladder tonic.

Siberian Ginseng Root stimulates the body's resistance to food or chemical sensitivities or allergies, and reduces fatigue and general weakness.

Milk Thistle Seed supports proper liver function and detoxification.

Calendula Extract contains therapeutic properties that address sensitive and irritated digestive tissues, including the stomach and intestinal lining, as well as the liver, gall bladder, spleen, and pancreas. It supports recovery from digestive upset due to hairballs.

Cascara Sagrada Bark, *Barberry Root*, *Senna Leaves*, *Rhubarb Root*, and *Cayenne* are all beneficial herbs that effectively clean the sensitive feline intestinal tract. A detoxified colon is fundamental to re-balancing the digestive system and increasing assimilation of nutrients necessary for proper health. These herbs can also prevent or reverse parasitic infestation.

Fennel Seed, *Ginger Root*, and *Anise Seed* can help relieve gas, cramping, and mucus while stimulating proper digestion and peristalsis.

IMMUNE SYSTEM DYSFUNCTION

Immune System Dysfunction often gives birth to chronic conditions. It is the result of a toxic lifestyle and glandular imbalance. It is vital that you address and support your cat's immune function. Unfortunately, it is not uncommon to see cats develop more serious dis-ease, such as cancer in its many forms (organ, blood, tissue, or bone), years after struggling with chronic symptoms associated with poor nutrition, improper digestion, "allergies," reoccurring infections, organ problems, and arthritis.

Many people have reported the increase or sudden development of cancer after their cat had been treated medically for another condition, such as a kidney problem. Although cancer is fast becoming the number-one killer of our cats today, I still see it as a symptom and recommend that it be treated as such. The best way to reverse cancer, including FIP and feline leukemia, is to strengthen the immune system.

Vitamins C, A, B-Complex and *E* cannot be surpassed for their immune-enhancing capabilities. Several other vitamins, amino acids, and minerals, such as *Zinc*, *Selenium*, and *Chromium* will also enhance immunity. It is important to seek a properly balanced and therapeutically potent multiple vitamin and mineral supplement.

In addition, several herbal and homeopathic remedies can improve the body's resistance to allergens or infections, reduce catabolic waste (responsible for many skin and digestive symptoms), and eliminate damaged or mutated cells that often lead to the development of cancerous cells and a weakened immune response.

Herbal extracts, preferably organic and standardized (those with a stronger, guaranteed potency), should be diluted in purified water or apple juice and given on an empty stomach, for optimum therapeutic response. Some cats may prefer tuna water or chicken stock to apple juice or water. If your cat is suffering from digestive disorders, herbs may be better tolerated when given with meals.

Immune-enhancing herbs include:

Sheep Sorrel, Burdock Root, Slippery Elm, and *Turkey Rhubarb Root* is an old tribal herbal combination for eliminating catabolic waste and stimulating the immune system. Chronic cases often need this foundation for deeper detoxification and a increased resistance to infection. Cats who suffer chronic weaknesses often fail to recover optimum wellness until this combination is introduced.

Garlic, Echinacea, and *Golden Seal Root* are nature's antibiotics, and have proven effective in combating viral, bacterial, yeast, and fungal infections—while stimulating the immune system in general. This combination cleans the blood, lymph system, liver, and kidneys. Other than garlic, it can be used topically for the reversal of abscesses, gangrene, and pus. It also can open blocked tear ducts. Please note that *Golden Seal* may be too strong an herb to give to severely weakened cats, especially those suffering from FIP or leukemia.

Astragalus Root helps tone and stimulate the spleen (an important immune system organ) to fight infection. It helps restore appetite, reduces fatigue, and lessens the diarrhea resulting from infection. It is useful for prolapsed conditions of the anus and impacted anal glands. It functions as a diuretic to flush wastes, reduce edema, and promote the discharge of pus. It also increases metabolism and aids the adrenals.

Pau d'Arco is beneficial for the whole body. It stimulates the immune system, heals wounds, and combats infections. It also kills viruses, and is effective against cancers (including leukemia), lupus, cysts, and benign tumors. Use it both internally and topically for ringworm, hot spots, eczema, psoriasis, and staphylococcal infections. It is excellent for the general support and reversal of cystitis, colitis, gastritis, diabetes, and liver and kidney weaknesses. It relieves arthritic pain and is easier on very sick, weakened, or older cats to tolerate than *Golden Seal Root*.

Lomatium Root, Echinacea Root, Spilanthes, Chinese Schizandra Berry, and Licorice Root in combination has strong antiviral and immune-enhancing properties. It targets cellular immunity and liver function to protect healthy cells from antigens and viral infection. It is especially indicated in cases of chronic viral infections that have not responded well to medications, or where the liver may be inflamed. It supports recovery (and reduces damage to other organ systems) from early manifestations of FIP, feline leukemia, upper respiratory disease, including rhinotracheitis or distemper. It can be used with *Astragalus* for debilitating or chronic infection.

Echinacea, Red Root, Baptisia Root, Thuja Leaf, and Prickly Ash Bark as a combination can remove toxins from the blood and lymphatic systems, while activating the body's immune response. It is a beneficial formula for conditions associated with immune breakdown that can be difficult to address by other methods. Other symptoms that respond well to this combination include anything that manifests as a result of catabolic waste build-up: tiny blood blisters, pimples/feline acne, mange, skin or mouth ulcerations, lymphatic engorgement, chronic infection, tumor growth, cysts, fluid cysts, and wasting disease. It can prevent or reverse late stage manifestations of cancer, including FIP and feline leukemia.

Spilanthes Leaf and Root, Grape Root, Juniper Berry, Usnea Lichen, and Myrrh Gum combined are very powerful anti-fungal and anti-yeast agents. These herbs have proven beneficial in reducing *Coccidioides immitis* (Valley Fever) spore infestation. This combination also helps the immune system respond to yeast overgrowth, vaginal infection, penis discharge, and ringworm.

Homeopathic remedies can facilitate the immune system's response to a specific toxin, allergen, bacterial, viral, or yeast infections, or parasitic infestation, although they should never be relied upon solely to address immune imbalance. If an animal is so debilitated, you may have no other choice but to use a homeopathic remedy. Otherwise, nutritional and herbal supplementation should be used as well. I have seen tremendous improvement in the immune system when I have included these remedies into the protocol.

Homeopathic remedies for immune stimulation include the following:

Arsenicum quickly triggers detoxification and elimination through the liver and kidneys, as well as stimulates other vital organs and glands that are responsible for proper immune response. *Arsenicum* prepares the body to utilize other therapeutic ingredients.

Gelsemium is an outstanding remedy for the first signs of dis-ease, especially fever. It is perfect for those pets who seem very needy and want to be held when they begin to feel sick, and also for those pets who have had a relapse after a long, debilitating illness and a weak recovery. It is an excellent feline leukemia remedy.

Iodum is appropriate for the first stages of liver, spleen, or pancreatic disease. It is also beneficial for initial thyroid or adrenal gland dysfunction. *Iodum* reduces glandular swelling with goiters.

Echinacea is good for irritated bowels and lymphatic engorgement. It helps address the fatigue often experienced during immune deficiencies, and is beneficial for cats with FIP.

Sweet Chestnut is a flower remedy that addresses deep despair and anguish often experienced by a cat after a long illness.

Flower "rescue" combinations should be used for overall support and immune stimulation when physical or emotional stress is present.

NEUROLOGICAL SYSTEM

Neurological disorders can be very frustrating to deal with. Many training problems and bad behaviors stem from an underlying neurological imbalance. Toxicity, either from viral infection or chemical exposure, should be suspected in these cases, since the ensuing irritation to the brain and nervous system may quickly manifest in many symptoms. Damage to the nerves through structural or traumatic impact can result in mobility problems. Brain damage, from accident or blunt trauma, can trigger encephalitis (inflammation), resulting in seizures and pain. Even feline leukemia or AIDS, which are often fatal, has been successfully reversed using holistic care and can even be prevented through the use of holistic animal care and homeopathic nosodes.

Epilepsy (seizures) is now quite genetically common, especially among popular breeds or mixes of Siamese, Persian, and Abyssinian cats. It should be noted that all cats are prone to epileptic seizures from ingested chemicals, viral infections, or trauma to the brain. I believe that yearly vaccinations, especially that aggressive kitten vaccination schedule, are more responsible for triggering seizures than the veterinary community is willing to acknowledge at this time. Recently, university studies concluded that the feline leukemia vaccine was not only ineffectual in over forty percent of vaccinated cats, but also frequently triggered neurological problems including seizures and paralysis.

There are so many other possible triggers for seizures, including sensitivity to yeast and urea, that I would suggest that we look deeper for a proper diagnosis. I believe that the usual diagnosis of epilepsy is often too freely determined, and pets are often unnecessarily drugged, leaving them prone to other diseases.

Epileptic seizure activity in felines is unpredictable with no set pattern or warning system. Some cats suffer frequent attacks, others more occasional ones. Heavy anti-convulsion drugs are often prescribed, which have debilitating side-effects. Regardless of the cause, seizure activity can be reversed through a natural approach. Supplement with additional high-quality *B-Complex Vitamins, Vitamin E*, and the amino acid *l-Tryptophan* (1500 mg. daily—regardless of size).

Homeopathically, I have had success reversing seizure activity with the following remedies:

Absinthium addresses seizures with twitching and trembling, especially when preceding the episode, or when seizures are coming in small clusters.

Silica addresses seizures that occur when the cat is resting or as the cat wakes up.

Belladonna is helpful for nausea or vomiting that follows a fit.

Thuja should be used when vaccinations are the suspected antecedent.

Arnica/Hypericum, combined, works wonders in reversing seizures related to trauma, such as car accidents.

Bioplasma, a combination of the twelve *tissue cell salts*, should be incorporated into daily supplementation for general support. You should add at least 100 mg. of *B-Complex Vitamins* per day, regardless of size, to rehabilitate the nervous system.

Herbal supplementation can quickly reverse the underlying hormonal and stress-related imbalance triggering the fits. Utilize an herbal combination of *Skullcap*, *St. John's Wort*, *Chamomile Flowers*, *California Poppy*, *Wild Oats*, and *Valerian Root*. This combination will help normalize and restore the nervous system. It will also make the cat calmer and reduce seizure activity, regardless of its cause. This formulation will not cause the sludgy side-effects of drugs; indeed, it has successfully weaned many cats off of the heavy narcotics used for seizure elimination. It allows them to live seizure-free *and alert* enough to enjoy their lives.

Feline Hyperesthesia Syndrome or Twitchy Skin Syndrome is a condition characterized by a rippling of the skin on a cat's back, especially when they lick or are petted in the lower back region. Some veterinarians feel that this is a form of epilepsy. I believe this condition may be caused by food additives and chemicals. Because this "weird behavior" is most often seen in high-strung cats such as Siamese and Himalayans, it is often considered to be a behavioral disorder. Chemical sedatives or progestin compounds are often prescribed for this condition, but this means of treatment is often unsuccessful. Calming and hormone-balancing natural remedies used for epilepsy can quickly reverse the behaviors associated with this condition.

Paralysis or muscular weakness can be caused by a reaction to a specific agent—a viral, bacterial, or fungal infection, yeast, pollen, food by-products, chemicals, or medication. It may also have a neurological origin. Any of these causes may result in defective or damaged nerves. After you get a proper diagnosis from your veterinarian, you can use nutritional, herbal, and homeopathic remedies to reduce inflammation, pain, and debility. Often a course of holistic treatment can result in complete reversal of reactive paralysis and significant improvement in neurological-based symptoms.

Homeopathic *Aconite*, when given with *Arsenicum*, is the best remedy to use for the initial onset of paralysis. Give it in frequent doses—it will provide initial relief of many symptoms. Taper off to two daily doses until recovery is complete. Use *Bufo* instead (or alternate with *Aconite*), if the initial onset follows severe arthritic symptoms. *Hypericum* is indicated when nerve involvement is suspected. *Carbo Veg.* is indicated for pets who *act* paralyzed, yet have no clinical symptoms (they have reflexes, etc.). This remedy is especially helpful if chronic disorders and a severe acute flare-up precede general symptoms of paralysis.

Strokes can come on suddenly from a variety of causes. Symptoms can be minor at first, but the cat's overall condition can rapidly deteriorate. Often strokes become frequent occurrences until the cat is totally debilitated. It is interesting that strokes in cats are very similar to those in humans. However, we do not know how much they are related.

The obvious symptoms are a pulling of the head to one side, droopy eyelids, and twitching. The cat may walk around in circles or get stuck in a corner and just sit and stare. Partial paralysis, especially of the mouth, because it makes eating and drinking difficult, requires more home care. *Aconite* is a good homeopathic remedy for strokes in general. Use *Bufo* if paralysis is the result of a stroke.

The best rehabilitative protocol for strokes is daily nutrients. Regardless of your cat's size, use *Vitamin B-Complex* (100 mg.), and *Vitamin E* (200 IUs for the first ten days, then reduce to 25 to 50 IUs per day) and the amino acids, *Selenium* (25 mcg.) and *l-Tryptophan* (1500 mg.). Rely on herbal and homeopathic remedies for other specific symptoms.

Yucca Root, in the standardized extract form only, is as effective as corticosteroids in most cases where anti-inflammatory support is needed. *Yucca* can even be used in conjunction with steroids to reduce the need for heavy doses of this potentially harmful medication, until the cat can be weaned solely onto the herb for long-term maintenance.

Vestibular Disease is a severe disorder of that part of the nervous system responsible for the maintaining balance and coordination of muscle activity. Chemicals, infectious diseases, trauma, and chronic ear infections can contribute to symptoms including head tilting or rolling, disorientation, vomiting, and falling over when attempting to walk. Genetically, Burmese and Siamese kittens are prone to developing *congenital vestibular syndrome* within the first month after birth. In these kittens, the part of the neuromuscular system responsible for proper gait does not develop properly. Siamese kittens with this condition will often be deaf as well, but will recover some motor coordination by six months old. However, Burmese kittens with this condition will not gain motor abilities and it is often necessary to euthanize the affected kittens. Providing nutritional support, including tissue cell salts, to the queen during gestation is vital to the prevention of this condition.

Vestibular ataxia syndrome can occur in kittens born to a queen who is stricken with feline parvovirus during pregnancy.

Kittens may have difficulty learning to walk, and the condition may or may not get worse over time. Holistic nosodes and remedies for structural inflammation or viral conditions may reverse these weaknesses.

HEART, BLOOD, AND THE CIRCULATORY SYSTEM

Anemia is a common symptom in chronically suffering cats. I believe that many cases of anemia arise from liver complications. Common symptoms of anemia include lack of stamina, a depressed appetite, poor coat condition with slow tissue repair, poor immune function, muscle weakness, washed-out gums, and dull eyes. Sometimes you can smell the faint odor of metal on the cat's breath. More serious anemia needs proper diagnosis and treatment, but borderline anemia is commonly reversed with proper nutrition.

Iron supplementation, a well-known treatment for anemia, will quickly reverse symptoms. Always use a good-quality source such as an iron proteinate (where the iron has been chelated and combined with an amino acid) for superior absorption. Be careful not to overdo iron supplementation, as it can easily become toxic. The first symptom of toxicity is constipation. Limit daily levels to around 10 mg. per day. In addition, provide *Chromium* to help iron assimilation. It reduces the need for higher levels of iron. I also utilize *Alfalfa*, both in herbal (nutrient-rich) or lower-potency homeopathic form. *Taraxacum 30C* is also a good homeopathic choice as is its herbal twin, *Dandelion*.

Avoid feeding your cat tuna on a regular basis. It can lead to anemia. Also avoid feeding liver on a regular basis. Although liver is a popular remedy for anemia, it is a primary detoxifying organ in an animal's body and stores many of the toxins it has eliminated from the blood. When you feed your cat liver, you are also feeding her concentrated toxins, including growth hormones and antibiotics.

Heart—Problems like a rapid heartbeat can accompany chronic allergy or arthritic reactions with powerful surges of histamine and adrenaline which stress the heart. Or such heart problems may be the result of years of improper diet and chemical use. Be sure to report any changes in your cat's breathing patterns or any weakness with exercise to your veterinarian. If heart problems are diagnosed, then nutritional supplementation with *Vitamin B-Complex*, *Vitamin E*, *Taurine*, *Selenium*, *Chromium*, and *Zinc*, as well as *Hawthorne Berries*, can help strengthen the heart muscle and regulate heart function.

Homeopathic remedies can quickly address acute symptoms, as well as stimulate an underlying reversal of debility when used on a long-term basis. Such remedies include:

Digitalis Purpurea is indicated after an attack in which the cat collapses as the result of exertion, often with the gums and tongue turning blue. Generally the pulse or heart rate may be abnormally slow. There may be a history of liver problems and fluid retention. Use 10X twice a day for two weeks following an attack, then dose with a 30C weekly to reduce the likelihood of a reoccurrence. Many cats have lived years after a serious attack, with the help of this remedy.

Aconite is beneficial when labored breathing and tumultuous heart action follows an allergic or emotional response, or when heart inflammation is suspected.

Iodum reduces acute heart inflammation. It can be combined with *Arsenicum*.

Arsenicum is indicated when weakness is triggered by a chemical reaction, particularly by vaccination, topical skin treatment, or pest control product. The heart may experience fluctuations between rapid and labored beating.

Calcarea fluorica should be used as a regular tissue cell salt supplement, as it can strengthen a dilated heart with a weak pulse.

Cardiomyopathy unfortunately is more common in cats today than it was in the past. Cats who are fed insufficient amounts of Taurine, who are fed chemicals, or who are subjected to other physical stresses are developing this condition. Siamese, Burmese, and Abyssinian cats tend to develop disorders of the heart muscle more than other breeds. The heart muscle can degenerate either through a thickening of the walls of the heart, which restricts blood flow, or through a thinning of the muscle tissue, which makes normal contractions impossible. Early symptoms include increased lethargy and appetite loss, followed later by coughing, breathing difficulties, physical collapse, and vomiting. The use of homeopathic *Digitalis* is beneficial in stabilizing the heart initially.

Arterial Thromboembolism, the development of large blood clots, can be the result of chronic *Cardiomyopathy*. Hind limb weakness, because the area is deprived of blood and oxygen, can be the primary symptom. *Nitricum Acidum* combined with homeopathic *Digitalis* can help resolve this condition.

Heartworms are a serious parasitic infestation of the blood. This can be a fatal infestation, both from the heartworms that clog the heart, and from the chemical cure. If the drug's side-effects don't kill the pet, the dead worms may block the heart so that it can't function. Prevention is definitely the best cure. Homeopathic nosodes (preventative and rehabilitative) have proven to be reliable. (See Parasites.)

Circulation is often slowed down by inflammatory responses, fluid retention, and heart conditions. Other than proper nutrition and detoxification, herbal and/or homeopathic *Cayenne* can greatly stimulate circulation.

Homeopathic remedies that work well on specific circulatory symptoms include:

Belladonna has marked action on the vascular system—especially with cats who are often frightful or aggressive, or who lack appetite and stamina, or who are sluggish.

Calcarea Phos. is an important tissue cell salt for poor circulation. Cats with poor circulation are often overweight. Their mouths and feet may feel cold to the touch.

Phosphorus is indicated for any internal bleeding.

Iberis is beneficial for an excitable cat with heart or circulatory problems..

THE URINARY SYSTEM

It is very important to pay attention to urinary problems. F.U.S. or Feline Urological Syndrome is one of the most diagnosed diseases in cats today. Your cat must be fed a proper diet and have free access to drinking water. He has to be able to urinate when he needs to. Holding urine in the bladder for extended periods of time leads to bacteria and crystal build-up. Urine flushes waste out of the body.

Urological Disorders *(especially F.U.S.)* are common in cats that have been fed poor-quality diets, given long-term medications, or who have suffered from chronic disease. As the body attempts to eliminate toxins, the urinary tract can become irritated and even blocked with bacteria or mineral crystals. Chemical poisoning or severe infection can further damage the kidneys.

Low-protein diets with additional salt (to encourage drinking) are often the prescribed course of treatment. Yet this may actually place an additional burden upon the body. Because the body is losing protein due to the kidney disease (since damaged organs leak protein), it needs a high-quality bio-available protein. Otherwise, the body will turn on itself, and use its own muscles as a protein source. This accounts for the "wasting disease" common with kidney failure. Detoxification can often clear up this chronic condition, but additional support may be needed. *Vitamin C* (a minimum of 1000 mg. per day) will acidify the urine, greatly reducing bacterial infection and kidney stone formation. Often minerals, such as calcium and magnesium, are restricted—but this can cause the body to store these minerals (as stones!). Proper mineral supplementation can actually decrease this storage.

Herbal care can strengthen and tone the bladder and kidneys, encourage urine output, and eliminate blockages and infection. Try the following herbs:

Juniper Berry, Spring Horsetail, Corn Silk, and *Goldenrod Leaf*, combined, can stimulate proper urine production and flow, eliminate toxins, reduce obstruction and stone formation, and soothe irritated membranes. The disinfecting properties of this combination will also help to reduce infection.

Usnea Lichen, Uva Ursi Leaf, Pipsissewa Herb, Echinacea Angustifolia and Purpurea Roots, Flowers, and Seeds are very fast-acting and powerful antibiotics for urinary tract infections associated with cystitis and nephritis. Certain therapeutic agents are known to target the bacteria responsible for urinary irritation and inflammation. This herbal combination is safe for long-term treatment and crisis care in older or more debilitated pets. It can be used safely with prescribed antibiotics, and it is especially useful when weaning a cat off of chronic drug use. You can use it to build up herbal properties while drugs attack more acute infection—so that when drugs have been discontinued, the herbs will continue to repair and protect the urinary tract in order to prevent the reoccurrence of the infection.

Yucca Extract acts as a general anti-inflammatory and is an alternative to steroids.

Homeopathic support can quickly address acute symptoms:

Arsenicum quickly addresses bladder and renal toxicity, especially from chemicals.

Cantharis or *Aconite* reduces irritation and pain during urination.

Thlaspi Bursa can quickly promote the flow of urine in cats who, because of the accumulation of gravel, have been urgently straining. It can often replace catheter use. It is beneficial when uric acid builds up from improper protein metabolism, and when phosphates are present in the urine as a result of poor kidney function.

Nux Vomica can help reduce nausea and restore lost appetite due to urinary tract problems. If toxicity is suspected, use it in combination with *Arsenicum*.

REPRODUCTIVE ISSUES
Spay and Neuter—It's the Only Way!

I have heard them all: "We want to show the kids the miracle of birth." "He'll get fat and lazy." Or even better, "Ouch, that *hurts me*!" These are all misconceptions about altering your cat. What is known is that spayed females are less likely to have mammary or uterine cancer, are less likely to run off, and are more likely to be healthy and happy. Neutered males are easier to train (although *no less* aggressive), are less likely to suffer from prostate cancer, are less likely to run off, and are more likely to live a more balanced, care-free life.

Although aggression is a learned behavior, cats who have the urge to reproduce can be difficult to house train, may embarrass you in front of company, and will tend to run off, getting into fights, car accidents—or worse, fall into the hands of someone who will abuse them. I highly recommend surgical birth control as a life-saving measure.

A few doses of homeopathic remedies can help your cat quickly recover from the operation with few side-effects. Use *Aconite, Hypericum, Arsenicum,* and *Nux Vomica* before and for a few day after surgery, in frequent doses throughout the day to address many related symptoms. *Phosphorus* can help to reduce bleeding. Flower combinations for "rescue" are also helpful, especially if your cat is anxious or fearful.

Reproduction can be difficult for cats who are toxic or who have suffered from chronic conditions. They often can not produce enough material (eggs, sperm, hormones, enzymes) to reproduce. Trust nature and stop trying to get them pregnant. *A healthy cat will easily reproduce.*

Please do not breed any cats with a history of poor health or emotional instability. It takes many generations to *breed out* a bad trait (if it is possible at all), so forget this angle unless you have twenty years and a lot of genetic research behind you. A trip to the shelter should quickly cure you of wanting to bring more kittens into this world, kittens who may never find a home, no matter how many friends you think will take one of them.

Pregnancy should be an easy process for both the mom and litter; especially if you and your cat are prepared. Proper care and support will ensure that everything will come out all right, or your cat will be better able to handle crisis if any problem should arise. Many cats first develop symptoms while they are pregnant. This is understandable, given the amount of toxins produced by supporting the growing litter. Some cats never have a reoccurrence of symptoms after the pregnancy. However, it is not uncommon to find that a cat's pregnancy was the onset of her chronic symptoms.

Because many herbs can be dangerous during pregnancy, please avoid the following: *White Willow Bark, Angelica, Golden Seal, Pennyroyal, Mugwort, Wormwood, Rue, Barberry, Cascara Sagrada, Buchu, Juniper,* or *Ephedra.*

In the event that you suspect your cat is exhibiting symptoms of pregnancy, utilize a well-balanced nutritional supplement with a potent *Vitamin B-Complex* and *C*. Also apply *safe* herbal remedies. You can rely on the effectiveness of homeopathic remedies as well at this time. No matter what you are doing, regardless even if you have been doing it before for your pet, be careful, and keep a close eye on the mother-to-be for any reactions to stress so that you can adjust her feeding and supplementation plan before there is a crisis. Afterbirth and discharge should be dark greenish-brown and odorless. The discharge should clear up within a day. If it becomes putrid-smelling or thickens, apply protocol for infections.

These are beneficial and safe homeopathic remedies for use during pregnancy:

Arsenicum, Apis, and *Nux Vomica* are safe for detoxification, digestive upsets, excessive licking, scratching, and skin eruptions; or for the reoccurrence of old symptoms.

Pulsatilla relieves reactive diarrhea during pregnancy, especially if your cat is highly excitable or suffers from exhaustion that is worse during the day. It is also good for the elimination of the placenta after birth; and it boosts milk production. A general female restorative, Pulsatilla both promotes the flow of milk at birth, and helps dry up the milk during weaning.

Phytolacca promotes milk production and flow. It is useful when the breasts are hard and painful.

Alumina is good for abnormal cravings, for a small, hard, knotty stool, or for difficulty passing a stool of any shape or consistency.

Phosphorus helps reduce uterine bleeding. It will settle a queen who gets anxious in early evening and seeks to hide from her kittens.

STRUCTURAL SYSTEM: MUSCLES, BONES, AND JOINTS

Arthritis is often used as a catch-all phrase to identify a wide variety of symptoms associated with muscle, bone, and joint disorders. These symptoms occur generally in conjunction with or as a direct reaction to certain conditions, especially those involving a congested or malfunctioning liver, kidneys, pancreas, and adrenal or thyroid gland.

Osteoarthritis, a degenerative joint disease, is a common condition in which the cartilage deteriorates or is defective. *Hip Dysplasia* is becoming a common form of degenerative joint disease in cats. Many cases of arthritis are caused by tissue damage rather than heredity. Improper nutrition, as well as old injuries from accidents or physical overexertion can also cause these conditions. Infectious arthritis, with its joint inflammation and pain, is caused by a bacterial or viral infection. Infectious arthritis can be a symptom of feline leukemia, and, if left untreated, can permanently damage cartilage and joints. Symptoms associated with this type of arthritis include fever and fatigue along with painfully swollen joints. Autoimmune disease can trigger arthritic conditions. Some cat breeds, such as Abyssinian, Exotic Short Hair, and Burmese, are more likely to suffer autoimmune-related arthritis, while systemic

Lupus (another autoimmune disease) seems to favor Siamese and the Oriental Short Hair cats.

The use of corticosteroids (anti-inflammatory agents) and pain medication may temporarily suppress arthritic symptoms, but will do little to repair the joint or to prevent further deterioration. Symptoms of arthritis and other structural conditions can best be suppressed *and possibly eventually reversed* homeopathically and/or herbally, while the joints, ligaments, muscles, and tendons are strengthened through nutritional supplementation. *Prevention is definitely possible.*

Osteomyelitis can be caused by a deep bite from another cat, which has infected bony tissue. Open fractures also predispose a cat to infection, while fungal or bacterial organisms can spread from other parts of the body via the blood. These cats become feverish and lame and often require surgery to remove affected bone mass. A holistically raised cat can reverse infections before they become serious.

The following structural or muscular conditions also respond well to holistic animal care, often eliminating the need for surgery or anti-inflammatory medications:

Cruciate knee ligament damage, tearing, or a severe sprain can occur in cats who have not been fed the best diet nor supplemented with adequate levels of *Vitamin C* (minimum 1000 mg. per day). Address acute ruptures with nutritional and herbal supplementation, and homeopathy to reverse weakness and pain.

Hip Dysplasia, a partial dislocation of the hip joints, is genetically passed down in some of the stout-bodied breeds of cats. Severe trauma, from a car accident, excessive exercise or jumping is often responsible for hip dislocation. Avoid encouraging your cat to overexert, jump too high—

especially straight up and down. Excessive rotation of the limb can damage the joint and tear ligaments. Never pull your kitten by the legs, and always limit exercise until they reach twelve months of age, the age when a cat's proper growth has been reached, and its structural and muscular systems have been strengthened.

Avoid encouraging or allowing kittens to run about too wildly, as this can trigger inflammation and pain. Do encourage movement and gradually increase play times to build up strength. The stronger you can build the connective tissue, the more stable the hip will remain within the joint, reducing the damage which leads to mobility difficulties, joint degeneration, calcification (from chronic bone repair), and pain.

Surgery is often sought out to stabilize the hip, but I have found that, unless total dislocation has occurred, it is not effective in the long run. Nutritional, herbal, and homeopathic remedies have provided more support and recovery in a high number of severe cases than I have seen through surgery.

High doses of *Vitamin C*, up to bowel tolerance, or at least 1000 mg. per day, can help to prevent hip dysplasia or at least slow down the degeneration and help relieve pain.

Metabolic Bone Disease results in a thinning and loss of bone tissue. This leaves the cats predisposed to fractures, growth deformities, and bone cancer. *Mucopolysaccharidoiss* is a common condition in which an enzyme deficiency leads to abnormal bone growth and tissue loss. This condition occurs frequently in Siamese cats (due to a genetic anomaly), and increases the likelihood of bone cancer. *Boron* is a vital supplement for this condition. Herbs, including *Red Root, Thuja Leaf, Blue Flag Root*, and *Baptisia Root*, are helpful in reducing bone tissue loss. *Echinacea* stimulates and balances the immune system and prevents the infection from settling deeper.

Myositis triggers inflammation of the muscle tissue, resulting in stiffness, pain, weakness, and eventual muscle atrophy. Partial, short-term paralysis is not uncommon after acute bouts.

Hypokalemia, a disease which affects the heart muscle and can cause lack of coordination, eating difficulty, and weight loss, is a common side-effect of potassium deficiency, and can trigger myositis. Infectious states, including some parasitic infestation, can also trigger the symptoms, which are best treated individually as symptoms, rather than as a disease. Herbs, especially *St. John's Wort* and *Valerian Root*, can relax muscular stress. Massage, acupuncture, and gentle exercise can also help strengthen the muscular system and greatly improve mobility and flexibility.

Patellar Luxation is similar to hip dysplasia, but it is localized within the knee. Improper nutrition has left the ligaments that surround and stabilize the knee weakened and vulnerable to injury or degeneration. Follow the recommendations for hip dysplasia and cruciate.

The following homeopathic remedies are highly effective in reversing acute or chronic symptoms associated with bone, joint, or muscular disorders:

Arsenicum is an excellent general arthritic and pain remedy.

Arnica reduces swelling, general muscular pain, and discomfort. It is good for trauma.

Bryonia helps the cat who is stiff upon getting up and *cannot* walk out of it.

Rhus Tox is for the cat who is stiff upon getting up but *can* walk out of it.

Hypericum reduces nerve irritation and pain common in cats who are constantly licking their legs and feet, and sometimes even their backs.

Ruta is best for severe tendon or ligament strains, common in nutritionally depleted cats. This herb has repaired the cruciate ligament, which is often so severely damaged that surgical correction is required. However, if the ligament is still sufficiently attached, this herb can regenerate tissue.

I recommend the following herbal remedies:

Yucca is a very effective anti-inflammatory. The stalk and roots contain steroidal saponins, which react in the body as chemical steroids would, but without the side-effects, to effectively reduce tissue inflammation and pain. *Yucca* encourages a range of motion which will keep the joint from freezing up. Be sure to use a cold-pressed extract, rather than a powder or tincture. The extract contains up to eighty-five percent more bio-available saponins than other forms, and it is easier on the digestive tract.

Garlic is a wonderful supplement for inflamed joints.

Milk Thistle, Licorice, Alfalfa, and *Dandelion* are all excellent remedies for liver and blood detoxification. They can reduce free radicals that may irritate joints.

Nutritionally supplement with the following:

Vitamin C will help reduce inflammation, strengthens ligaments and tendons, and reduces allergy sensitivities. It is an excellent antioxidant and is the number one vitamin for healthy joints and ligaments.

MSM, a sulfur-based product, not only helps reduce inflammation, but is also good for poor skin and coat conditions.

Antioxidants such as *Selenium, Grapeseed Extract, SOD,* and *Vitamin E* reduce inflammation.

Glucosamines help replenish synovial fluid, an imbalance of which can create the rubbing of bone upon bone, resulting in pain and encouraging calcium build-up—the repercussion of which is worse arthritis.

Boron helps with calcium absorption and strengthens bone density. It helps to avoid build-up of calcium or over-calcification, as found in arthritic conditions.

PARASITES

Parasites can seriously compromise the body, interfering with proper digestion and assimilation, and leaving the body more susceptible to imbalance and dis-ease. Parasitic infestation can become deadly: Infection can set in and organ failure can occur. You must keep your cat free of infestation.

Intestinal Worms—If you suspect intestinal worms, because there are chronic stool problems, with evidence of mucous-covered rice or string-like bodies (especially if the stool wiggles!), apply a sound herbal worming program immediately. If, within two weeks, you have not eliminated them, seek veterinarian support. Avoid chemical worming preparations whenever possible. These can be so harsh that they can permanently damage the sensitive lining of the digestive tract of young animals.

Herbal worming can be successful if you follow the directions carefully. Often, the products need to be administered along with fasting for optimum effect. Intestinal worms such as roundworms feed off of old fecal material backed up in the colon. These parasites cannot thrive in a clean, healthy gut. Look for products which contain herbs such as *Rhubarb Root*, which is especially effective against round and pinworms; *Cayenne*, which helps eliminates eggs; *Barberry Root, Senna Leaves, Wormwood, Quassia Bark* (this works well on

Giardia), *Black Walnut Hulls, Neem*, or *Bilva herb* (excellent general dewormers).

Heartworms, as well as other blood parasites, can be addressed with this combination, although some worms can be fatal, so be sure to seek veterinary support. Homeopathic heartworm nosodes are available and have been proven to be good for the elimination and prevention of infestation. *Hawthorne* and *Garlic* are excellent herbs for heart rehabilitation.

Skin Parasites can trigger your cat's chronic symptoms, especially chronic skin eruptions or infections. It is prudent to have your cat carefully examined for skin parasites in order to find out if they are the source of your pet's symptoms. Avoid the use of medicated or chemical-based topical pest control treatments, which could possibly compromise the immune system and increase your cat's sensitivity to toxins.

Regardless of your findings, the immune system imbalance remains the fundamental issue that needs to be addressed, since pests do not generally invade non-toxic cats. Waste products being exuded through the skin invite and feed fleas and ticks. Yeast, commonly used to ward off these pests, may become toxic to the liver, increasing instances of infestation. Yeast also promotes ear wax and debris, which will provide a birthing area for bacterial and yeast infections, which in turn can attract ear mites.

Mites are vicious skin parasites that burrow down into the epidermis, causing *Mange*, which prompts a great deal of discomfort and irritation. Scratching and chewing can quickly lead to an infection with discharge. Mange can be widespread on the body, but often remains localized in the head and neck region, where it causes skin inflammation and spreading patterns of rashes and hair loss. Treat it topically daily with a solution of twelve drops of *Grapefruit Extract*, six drops each of *Tea Tree Oil*, *Golden Seal Root Extract*, and *Pau d'Arco Extract*, two drops of *Yucca Extract*, three tablespoons fresh squeezed *lemon juice* diluted in two ounces of *Witch Hazel*, and four ounces of distilled water. Let air dry and leave area uncovered.

Ear Mites or Otodectes are tiny, white, spider-like pests, that are practically impossible to see with the naked eye. They leave debris resembling finely ground pepper, resulting in a gritty discharge. To dissolve a suspected infestation, follow my recommendations for removal of an object from the ear. Allow the ear oil to set for as long as your pet will tolerate it, at least one-half hour to suffocate the mites. Finish by massaging the base to loosen the debris further before flushing the ear with a cleaning solution. Repeat several times per day until all the mites are removed, usually within a day or two.

Fleas and Ticks can create a lot of problems for the skin, and, if infestation is allowed to continue, it will make treating chronic symptoms impossible. These pests are not only weakening your cat, they can infect her with a more serious disease. *Diatomaceous Earth* is tiny, ground-up fossils which dehydrate the pest's outer coating, killing it. This earth can provide an effective barrier between your home or yard and the pests. Clean your cat and her bedding well with a natural insecticide shampoo and follow with a natural dip. Follow the directions carefully. Groom your pet every day to help remove pests, along with dead skin. This will make skin treatments easier. Remember to feed garlic!

Ringworm is a fungal infection. It can also create a lot of the symptoms associated with allergies, such as skin inflammation, itching, and hot spots. Ringworm is evidenced by a small, circular area which is bare of hair and very irritated. Your pet may scratch at it, causing a bacterial infection. Treat it topically with mange solution or apply some lavender oil.

Seek additional specific herbal or homeopathic support, according to symptoms, when needed. *Red Clover Blossoms, Stinging Nettle Leaf, Cleavers Herb, Yellow Dock Root, Burdock Root, Yarrow Flowers, Plantain Leaf and Corm, Licorice Root,* and *Prickly Ash Bark* are excellent herbs to use for skin disorders such as mange. *Spilanthes Leaf and Root, Grape Root, Juniper Berry, Usnea Lichen,* and *Myrrh Gum* can be used together effectively to reverse ringworm, as can *Sarsaparilla* (both can be used topically and internally). Homeopathic *Tellurium* is a primary ringworm remedy, especially when the eczema is localized behind the ears and neck. In a pinch, *Arsenicum* can work as well on most skin parasitic-related cases.

How to Be Your Vet's Best Friend

The most important ally that you can have, in taking care of your pet, is a trusted veterinarian. You should never think that you can handle each and every health concern on your own. You can however, manage your pet's health care yourself, while making all medically-related decisions using the expertise and guidance of a competent professional. Rely on your veterinarian to explain specific genetic weaknesses and local health concerns so that you can develop a sound preventative program around your pet's individual needs.

Yearly health exams and occasional blood work can help catch an imbalance early, before it becomes a health problem. Often an imbalance in the endocrine system, protein assimilation, or blood sugar irregularities can be spotted long before the actual symptoms, such as allergies or organ failure, show themselves. This can make the difference between simply reversing an acute weakness or having a chronic condition develop. Proper diagnosis to verify a specific imbalance can make the difference between addressing the problem head-on and more successfully, or trying a "hit or miss" therapy that can go on for months. Monitoring the body as it responds to the chosen therapy will also help you identify generally what is, or isn't, working.

Today, there are more holistically-oriented veterinarians who are well versed in the complementary modalities of nutritional therapy, herbs, homeopathy, acupuncture, massage and chiropractic care. Some have even expanded to incorporate esoteric therapies of sound, light and energy healing. In addition, a large number of allopathic (traditionally trained) veterinarians now realize that natural pet care has its place within their traditional, medically-based treatments.

Unfortunately, many of us have had very negative experiences with veterinarians—especially those allopathically trained veterinarians who are unfamiliar with natural care and thus are uncompromising. We may now avoid seeking veterinary support. Possibly, they have spoken to us as if we did not have a clue in our heads about our pet's health care needs, or dismissed our attempts to seek a chemical-free lifestyle for our pets. More likely, they simply failed to address past conditions successfully, and we have lost faith in the medical approach. I am hoping that by giving you a little insight as to what can be successfully accomplished with natural modalities, while encouraging you to join forces with your veterinarian—rather than give them unchallenged authority over your pet's medical care—will help empower you so that you can successfully incorporate proper veterinary care in your pet's holistic lifestyle.

It is vital that you seek a veterinarian who is willing to listen to you, is thorough in their examination and diagnosis, will explain what it is that they recommend and why—but most importantly—will treat you and your pet with respect. If you do not like the way a veterinarian approaches your pet or speaks to you, then find another no matter who recommended them.

It becomes very frustrating for a diagnostician when a pet owner doesn't have the most basic information, and puts the veterinarian (who cares) at a disadvantage—in properly identifying what might be at the bottom of the pet's symptoms. Soon, such veterinarians become jaded and assume that all their clients simply don't have a clue. Who can blame them? Open the lines of communication. Learn more about the choices you make and the recommendations given to you by all concerned parties. You know your pet best and this information will help your companion receive better veterinary care.

By making the necessary changes in their lifestyle and health care before a serious problem or chronic condition develops, you will keep them healthy. Prevention IS the best cure!

THE CROSSING PRESS POCKET PET SERIES

Allergies
By Lisa Newman
$6.95 • Paper • ISBN 1-58091-002-5

Arthritis
By Lisa Newman
$6.95 • Paper • ISBN 1-58091-003-3

Natural Dog
By Lisa Newman
$6.95 • Paper • ISBN 1-58091-001-9

Nutrition
By Lisa Newman
$6.95 • Paper • ISBN 1-58091-004-1

Parasites
By Lisa Newman
$6.95 • Paper • ISBN 1-58091-006-8

Skin & Coat Care
By Lisa Newman
$6.95 • Paper • ISBN 1-58091-008-4

Training without Trauma
By Lisa Newman
$6.95 • Paper • ISBN 1-58091-007-6